Bread Baker's Bible

Bread Baker's Bible

TRADITIONAL BREAD RECIPES
FROM AROUND THE WORLD

Jennie Shapter

southwater

This edition is published by Southwater

Distributed in the UK by
The Manning Partnership
251–253 London Road East
Batheaston
Bath BA1 7RL
UK
tel. (0044) 01225 852 727
fax. (0044) 01225 852 852

Distributed in the USA by
Ottenheimer Publishing
5 Park Center Court
Suite 300
Owing Mills MD 2117–5001
USA
tel. (001) 410 902 9100
fax. (001) 410 902 7210

Distributed in Australia by
Sandstone Publishing
Unit 1, 360 Norton Street
Leichhardt
New South Wales 2040
Australia
tel. (0061) 2 9560 7888
fax. (0061) 2 9560 7488

Distributed in New Zealand by
Five Mile Press NZ
PO Box 33–1071
Takapuna
Auckland 9
New Zealand
tel. (0064) 9 4444 144
fax. (0064) 9 4444 518

Southwater is an imprint of Anness Publishing Limited
© 1999, 2000 Anness Publishing Limited

1 3 5 7 9 10 8 6 4 2

PUBLISHER: Joanna Lorenz
EXECUTIVE EDITOR: Linda Fraser
EDITOR: Susannah Blake
DESIGNER: Nigel Partridge
PHOTOGRAPHERS: Nicki Dowey (recipes) and Amanda Heywood
HOME ECONOMIST: Jennie Shapter
EDITORIAL READER: Diane Ashmore
PRODUCTION CONTROLLER: Yolande Denny

Previously published as part of a larger compendium *The World Encyclopedia of Bread and Bread Making*

Contents

INTRODUCTION

There is something undeniably special about bread. The flavor of a good loaf, the texture of the soft crumb contrasting with the crispness of the crust, is almost a sensual experience. Who can walk home with a fresh baguette without slowly, almost absent-mindedly breaking the crust and picking off pieces to eat en route? Or resist the promise of a slice of a soft white farmhouse loaf, spread simply with butter? Most people have their own favorite: ciabatta, rich with olive oil; dark, malty rye; honeyed *challah* or a Middle Eastern bread, freshly baked and redolent of herbs and spices. Whatever the shape or texture, bread has a special place in our affections.

Even today, at the turn of the century, when bread is taken largely for granted, seen as an accompaniment or a "carrier" for other foods, we still have a sense of its supreme significance. In some languages the word "bread" means "food," and in certain of the more rural parts of Spain and Italy, for example, you may find that bread is blessed or kissed before being broken or eaten. There are numerous rituals and traditions attached to bread. Slashing the dough with a cross or making a sign of the cross over the loaf before baking was believed to let the devil out. Cutting the bread at both ends was also recommended to rid the house of the devil. One extraordinary custom was sin-eating, a

BELOW: Cutting a cross in an unbaked loaf was believed to let the devil out.

ABOVE: Just a few of the many shapes and types of bread.

practice at funerals, where someone would eat a loaf of bread and by so doing would take on the sins of the dead person.

The obvious explanation for bread's importance is that until quite recently, it was for many, quite literally the "staff of life"—the single essential food. Today, most people have more varied diets. Potatoes, pasta and rice are all enjoyed in the West and are important staple foods, but in some countries, France, Italy and Spain, for example, bread is easily the most popular of the carbohydrates, eaten with every meal and in many cases with every course.

Like wine tasters, true aficionados taste bread *au naturel* in order to savor its unique taste and texture, unadulterated by other flavors. Good as plain bread can be, the best thing about bread is that it goes so well with other foods. Throughout Europe bread is most frequently cut or broken into pieces to be eaten with a meal—to mop up soups and sauces or to eat with hams, pâtés and cheese. Dark rye breads, spread with strongly-flavored cheese or topped with smoked fish, are popular in northern Europe, and in the Middle East breads are split and stuffed with meats and salads—a tradition that has been warmly embraced in the West

too. In Britain and the United States, the European custom of serving bread with a meal, with or instead of potatoes or rice, is catching on, but sandwiches are probably still the favorite way of enjoying bread. Sandwiches have been going strong for a couple of hundred years—invented, it is said, by John Montagu, 4th Earl of Sandwich, so that he could eat a meal without having to leave the gaming table. Although baguettes and bagels are naturally suited for linking bread with meat, the sandwich, clearly an English concept, is unique and continues to be the perfect vehicle for fillings that become more and more adventurous.

BREADS OF TODAY

Figures show that throughout Europe bread consumption declined after World War II. Until then it was the single most important food in the diet, but due to increased prosperity, which meant a wider choice of other foods, and mass production, which led to bread becoming increasingly insipid and tasteless, people moved away from their "daily bread." The situation was more noticeable in some countries than others. In France, Italy and Spain, where people continued to demand the best, bread consumption did not decline so sharply, although even in these countries, the quality did deteriorate for

BELOW: In northern Europe, dark rye bread is served sliced with colorful, rich-tasting toppings.

a time. In Britain, however, most bread was notoriously bland—the ubiquitous white sliced loaf being little more than a convenient shape for the toaster. In supermarkets, certainly, there was a time, not so long ago, when other than the standard pre-wrapped white loaf, the only baked goods on sale were croissants and a selection of fruited teabreads, vaguely labeled as "Continental." Yet within the last ten years, things have improved by leaps and bounds. Perhaps supermarkets, finding that the smell of freshly baking bread enticed shoppers into their stores, installed more in-store bakeries. Or perhaps shoppers who traveled abroad and sampled the breads of other countries created a demand for better breads made with better flours, using more imaginative recipes and untreated with additives.

Nowadays there is a wide variety of breads available both from independent bakeries and large supermarkets. Italian ciabatta and focaccia are now a regular sight, even in the smallest food stores, as are various Spanish, Indian and Middle Eastern breads. There is an increasingly wide variety of German, Danish, Scandinavian and Eastern European breads and, among the French breads, there is now a truly good range. If the supermarket has an in-store bakery, baguettes are likely to be freshly baked, and some are now as good as the real thing. The availability of *pain de campagnes*, *levains* and other rustic breads means that you can choose breads to suit the style of meal you are serving, while sweet breads, such as brioches and croissants from France, *pane al cioccolato* from Italy and numerous offerings from Germany, mean that there is much more to choose from than simply toast at breakfast and rolls with dinner.

Local bakers, although competing with the supermarkets, have paradoxically benefited from the range available at supermarkets. The more breads there are available, the more people feel inclined to try other baked goods. Small bakers who could have easily lost customers to the big stores, have risen to the challenge by producing their own range of country-style and fine breads. Craft bakers are

ABOVE: A huge range of traditionally baked French breads are offered for sale at this specialty bakery.

producing traditional breads, at the same time experimenting with recipes they have devised themselves. Bread making has never been a tradition that stood still. The best craft bakers have ensured that bread making has continued to evolve, resulting in the emergence of all kinds of corn and barley breads, mixed grain loaves and a range of new sourdoughs.

Added to this are the many European-style bakeries. Set up and run by émigrés from all parts of Europe and beyond, these bakeries are the best source of many of the most authentic European breads. In supermarkets you will invari-

BELOW: Traditional country-style breads are enjoying a renaissance.

ably find ciabatta or focaccia, but for *paesano*, *pagnotta* or *pane sciocco* you are likely to need an Italian baker, who will be only too happy to provide you with the loaves and tell you all about them while they are being wrapped.

Once you have found a bakery you like, there are no particular tips for buying bread; the baker will be pleased to explain the different styles of loaves and advise on their keeping qualities. Crusty breads, such as baguettes and Italian country loaves are known as "oven bottom" or "oven bottom-baked," which means they have been baked, without pans or containers, on the bottom of the oven or on flat baking sheets or stones. They are evenly crusty, although the type of dough, the humidity during proving, the steam in the oven and the heat itself determines whether the crust is fragile or chewy. Loaves such as the English farmhouse ones, baked in metal pans, characteristically have a golden top, but with thinner crust on the sides. Rolls or breads baked packed up against each other have even softer sides and are described as "batch-baked." Sourdough breads are made without yeast —using a natural leaven instead—and are often labeled as "yeast-free" breads or "naturally leavened." There are many varieties, some made entirely from wheat, some from rye, others from a blend of both of these or other grains. They are normally heavier than an average loaf, with a dense texture and pleasantly tart flavor.

Ingredients for Bread Making

Wheat Flours

The simplest breads are a mixture of flour and water and some type of leavening agent. Beyond that narrow definition, however, lies an infinite number of possibilities. The flour is most likely to come from wheat, but may be derived from another type of grain or, even, in the case of buckwheat, from another source entirely. The liquid may be water, but could just as easily be milk, or a mixture. Yeast is the obvious raising agent, but there are other options. Salt is essential, fats are often added, and other ingredients range from sweeteners like sugar or molasses to dried fruit, spices and savory flavorings.

White Flour
This flour contains about 75 percent of the wheat grain with most of the bran and the wheat germ extracted. Plain flour is used for pastry, sauces and cookies, while self-rising flour, which contains a raising agent, is used for cakes, scones and other desserts. It can also be used for soda bread. American all-purpose flour is a medium-strength flour, somewhere between the British plain and strong white flour. Soft flour, sometimes known as American cake flour, has been milled very finely for sponge cake and similar baked goods.

Unbleached White Flour
Unbleached flour is more creamy in color than other white flours, which have been whitened artificially. Bleaching, which involves treating the flour with chlorine, is becoming increasingly rare and the majority of white flours are unbleached, although check the package to be sure. In Britain, flour producers are required by law to add, or fortify their white flours with certain nutrients such as vitamin B1, nictinic acid, iron and calcium. These are often added in the form of white soy flour, which has a natural bleaching effect.

RIGHT: Organic flours are being used increasingly for bread making.

Strong White/White Bread Flour
For almost all bread making, the best type of flour to use is one that is largely derived from wheat that is high in protein. This type of flour is described as "strong" and is often labeled "bread flour," which underlines its suitability for the task. It is the proteins that combine to form gluten when mixed with water, and it is this that gives dough its elasticity when kneaded, and allows it to trap the bubbles of carbon dioxide given off by the yeast. A soft flour produces flat loaves that stale quickly; conversely, if the flour is too hard, the bread will have a coarse texture. A balance is required and most millers blend hard and soft wheats to make a flour that produces a well-flavored loaf with good volume. Most strong white flours have a lower protein content than their whole-wheat equivalent and a baker would probably use a flour with a protein level of 12 percent. The protein value of a flour can be found listed on the side of the package under "Nutritional Value."

Fine French Plain Flour
French bakers use a mixture of white bread flour and all-purpose flour to make baguettes and other specialties. French all-purpose flour is called *farine fluide* in its country of origin because it is so light and free-flowing. Such is the popularity of French-style baked goods that this type of flour is now available in European supermarkets.

Whole-wheat Flour
This flour is made using the whole of the wheat grain and is sometimes called 100 percent extraction flour: nothing is added and nothing is taken away. The bran and wheat germ, which are automatically separated from the white inner portion if milled between rollers, are returned to the white flour at the end of the process. *Atta* is a fine whole-wheat flour used for Indian breads (see Other Flours).

Stoneground Whole-wheat Flour
This whole-wheat flour has been ground in the traditional way between two stones. The bran and wheat germ are milled with the rest of the wheat grain, so there is no separation of the flour at any stage. Stoneground flour is also considered to have a better flavor, owing to the slow grinding of the stones. However, because the oily wheat germ is squashed into the flour, rather than churned in later, stoneground flour has a higher fat content and may become rancid if stored for too long.

Organic Whole-wheat Flour
This flour has been milled from organic wheat, which is wheat produced without the use of artificial fertilizers or pesticides. There are organic versions of all varieties of whole-wheat and white flours available at most large supermarkets and health-food stores.

Strong Whole-wheat/ Whole-wheat Bread Flour
A higher proportion of high gluten wheat is necessary in whole-wheat flours to counteract the heaviness of the bran. If the flour is not strong enough, the dough may rise unevenly and is likely to collapse in the oven. The miller selects his grist (the blend) of hard and soft wheat grains, according to the type of flour required. Bakers would probably look for a protein content of about 13.5 percent; the strong flours available in supermarkets are normally between 11.5 and 13 percent.

ABOVE: A selection of different wheat flours and grains. Clockwise from top right: strong white flour, stoneground whole-wheat, whole-wheat, wheat germ, organic whole-wheat, plain flour, organic plain flour, semolina, organic stoneground whole-wheat and Granary flour. The three flours in the center are (clockwise from top) brown, spelt and self-rising flour.

GRANARY FLOUR

Granary is the proprietary name of a blend of brown and rye flours and malted wheat grain. The malted grain gives this bread its characteristic sweet and slightly sticky flavor and texture. It is available at health-food stores and supermarkets.

MALTHOUSE FLOUR

A specialty flour available at some large supermarkets and healthfood stores, this is a combination of stoneground brown flour, rye flour and malted wheat flour with malted wheat flakes. It resembles Granary flour.

GRAHAM FLOUR

This popular American flour is slightly coarser than ordinary whole-wheat. It is named after a 19th-century Massachusetts cleric, Reverend Sylvestor Graham, who developed the flour and advocated using the whole grain for bread making because of the beneficial effects of the bran.

BROWN FLOUR

This flour contains about 85 percent of the original grain, with some of the bran and wheat germ extracted. It produces a lighter loaf than 100 percent whole-wheat flour, while still retaining a high percentage of wheat germ, which gives bread so much of its flavor.

WHEAT GERM FLOUR

A wheat germ flour can be brown or white but must contain at least 10 percent added wheat germ. Wheat germ is highly nutritious and this bread is considered particularly healthy. Wheat germ bread has a pleasant nutty flavor.

SEMOLINA

This is the wheat kernel or endosperm, once the bran and wheat germ have been removed from the grain by milling, but before it is fully milled into flour. Semolina can be ground either coarsely or finely and is used for certain Indian breads, including *bhatura*.

SPELT

Although spelt, a variety of wheat, is no longer widely grown, some flour mills still produce a spelt flour, which is available at healthfood stores.

OTHER FLOURS

Alternative grains, such as barley, cornmeal and oatmeal, are full of flavor but contain little or no gluten. Breads made solely from them would rise poorly and would be extremely dense. The milled grains are therefore often mixed with strong wheat flour. Rye is rich in gluten, but pure rye doughs are difficult to handle; once again the addition of strong wheat flour can provide a solution.

BARLEY MEAL

Barley is low in gluten and is seldom used for bread making in Britain and western Europe. In Russia and Eastern European countries, however, barley loaves continue to be produced, the flour mostly blended with some proportion of wheat or rye flour to give the loaf volume. These loaves are definitely on the robust side. They tend to be rather gray and flat and have an earthy, rather mealy flavor. Similar loaves must have been baked in parts of the British Isles in the past, when times were hard or the wheat harvest had failed. There are several old Welsh recipes for barley bread, which was rolled out flat before being baked on a baking stone. Finnish barley bread is made in much the same way.

Barley meal is the ground whole grain of the barley, while barley flour is ground pearl barley, with the outer skin removed. Either can be added in small quantities to

BELOW: Finnish barley bread

whole-wheat or to white flour to produce a bread with a slightly rustic flavor.

BUCKWHEAT FLOUR

This grain is blackish in color, hence its French name, *blé noir*. It is not strictly a cereal but is the fruit of a plant belonging to the sorrel family. The three-cornered grains are milled to a flour and used for pancakes, blinis and, in France, for crêpes or galettes. It can also be added to wheat flour and is popular mixed with other grains in multigrained loaves. It has a distinctive, earthy flavor and is best used in small quantities.

CORNMEAL (MAIZEMEAL)

This meal is ground from white or yellow corn and is normally available in coarse, medium or fine grinds. Coarse-ground cornmeal is used for the Italian dish of polenta; for bread making, choose one of the finer grinds, available at most healthfood stores. There are numerous cornbreads from the southern United States, including cornbread made with fresh corn kernels. Corn was brought back to Europe by the Spanish and Portuguese and corn breads are still popular in these countries today, particularly in Portugal. Corn contains no gluten so will not make a loaf unless it is blended with wheat flour, in which case the corn adds a pleasant flavor and color.

MILLET FLOUR

Although high in protein, millet flour is low in gluten and is not commonly used by itself in bread making. It is pale yellow in color, with a gritty texture. The addition of wheat flour produces an interesting, slightly nutty flavor.

OATMEAL

Oatmeal does not contain gluten and is only very rarely used by itself for bread making. The exception is in Scotland where flat yeast-leavened oatmeal biscuits have been popular for centuries. These are baked on a griddle and served with butter or marmalade. Oatmeal can also be used in wheat or multigrain loaves. Choose finely ground oatmeal for making oatcakes or for using in loaves. Rolled oats are not a flour but are the steamed and flattened whole oats. They look good sprinkled on the crust of loaves and rolls, and add a pleasant flavor.

RICE FLOUR

Polished rice, if ground very finely, becomes rice flour. It can be used as a thickening agent and is useful for people with wheat allergies. It is also occasionally used for some Indian breads.

STORAGE

Although most flours keep well, they do not last indefinitely, and it is important to pay attention to the "use-by" date on the package. Old flour will begin to taste stale and will make a disappointing loaf. Always store flour on a cool dry shelf. Ideally, the flour should be kept in its bag and placed in a tin or storage jar with a tight-fitting lid. Wash and dry the jar thoroughly whenever replacing with new flour and avoid adding new flour to old. Whole-wheat flour, because it contains the oils in wheatgerm, keeps less well than white flours. Consequently, do not buy large quantities at a time and keep it in a very cool place or in the salad drawer of the refrigerator.

ABOVE: Panettone is enriched with eggs and egg yolks.

BELOW: Red lentil dosas are spiced with turmeric and black pepper.

FRUIT

Almost any dried fruit can be added to bread. Raisins, currants and mixed peel have always been popular for fruit loaves. Chopped dates, apricots and prunes can all be kneaded in, as can more exotic fruits, such as dried mango or papaya. Fruit can be added to a dough during mixing or left until the second kneading. If adding at the second kneading, warm the fruit first, so that it does not inhibit the action of the yeast. If you are using an electric mixer or food processor for kneading, note that the blades, particularly on the food processor, will chop the fruit. This spoils both the appearance and the flavor of the loaf, so only knead by machine to begin with, then knead the fruit in by hand after the initial rising.

FATS

Fats, in the form of butter, oil, lard or vegetable shortening, are sometimes added to savory loaves. They add flavor and help preserve the freshness of the loaf. The Italians particularly love adding olive oil to their breads, which they do in generous quantities. Although oils and melted butter can be poured into the flour with the yeast and liquid, solid butter or fats are normally kneaded into the flour before the liquid is added.

NUTS, HERBS AND OTHER SAVORY INGREDIENTS

Some of our favorite breads today are flavored with herbs, nuts and other

BELOW: Ciabatta, like many Italian breads, is made with olive oil.

such savory ingredients. *Manoucher,* "Mediterranean nights" bread, is a rainbow of colors. Based on the Italian *focaccia,* it contains rosemary, red, green and yellow bell peppers along with goat cheese. The Italians add olives or sun-dried tomatoes to their ciabatta, while walnut bread (*pain aux noix* in France, *pane con noci* in Italy) is one of the best-known and best-loved savory loaves.

Nuts, herbs, pitted olives and sun-dried tomatoes should be roughly chopped before being kneaded into the dough after the first rising.

SPICES

The sweet spices are cinnamon, nutmeg, cloves and ginger, and for savory breads cumin, fennel, caraway and anise impart a delicious flavor. Mace, pepper and coriander seeds can be used for both sweet and savory breads. Spices can be added with the flour or kneaded in with fruit or nuts, or other ingredients.

TECHNIQUES

USING YEAST

There are several different forms of yeast, some easier to use than others, but none of them particularly tricky if you follow a few simple rules. Whichever yeast you use, it must be in good condition—neither old nor stale—and must not be subjected to too much heat.

USING COMPRESSED CAKE YEAST

Compressed cake yeast is occasionally available at baker's stores, healthfood stores and gourmet supermarkets with in-store bakeries. It is pale beige in color, has a sweet, fruity smell and should crumble easily. It can be stored in the refrigerator, wrapped in plastic wrap for up to 2 weeks or frozen for up to 3 months. A quantity of ½ ounce should be sufficient for 6–8 cups flour, although this will depend on the recipe.

1 Put the yeast in a small bowl. Using a spoon, mash or "cream" it with a little of the measured water until smooth.

2 Pour in the remaining measured liquid, which may be water, milk or a mixture of the two. Mix well. Use as directed in the recipe.

USING ACTIVE DRIED YEAST

Active dried yeast is simply the dehydrated equivalent of fresh yeast, but it needs to be blended with lukewarm liquid before use. Store dried yeast in a cool dry place and check the "use-by" date on the package. You will need about ½ ounce (1½ teaspoons) active dried yeast for 6 cups flour. Some bakers add sugar or honey to the liquid to which the yeast is added, but this is not necessary, as the granules contain enough nourishment to enable the yeast to work.

1 Pour the measured lukewarm liquid into a small bowl and sprinkle the dried yeast evenly over the surface.

2 Cover with plastic wrap and let sit in a warm room for 10–15 minutes until frothy. Stir well and use as directed.

WATER TEMPERATURE
For fresh and regular dried yeast, use lukewarm water; for easy-blend and fast-action yeast the water can be a little hotter, as the yeast is mixed with flour before the liquid is added.

USING QUICK-RISE DRIED YEAST

This is the most convenient of the dried yeasts as it can be stirred directly into the flour. This yeast contains a bread improver, which eliminates the need for two kneadings and risings—check the instructions on the package to make sure. Most of these yeasts come in ¼-ounce envelopes, which are sufficient for 6 cups flour. Do not store opened envelopes as the yeast will deteriorate quickly.

Sift together the flour and salt into a medium bowl and rub in the fat, if using. Stir in the easy-blend or fast-action dried yeast, then add warm water or milk, plus any other ingredients, as directed in the recipe.

BELOW: Small, shaped rolls are very quick to make using easy-blend yeast.

MAKING A YEAST DOUGH BY THE SPONGE METHOD

This method produces bread with an excellent flavor and soft texture. The quantities listed are merely an example and can be increased proportionately. See individual recipes.

1 Mix ¼-ounce fresh yeast with 1 cup lukewarm water in a large bowl. Stir in 1 cup unbleached plain flour, using a wooden spoon, then use your fingers to draw the mixture together until you have a smooth liquid with the consistency of a thick batter. (Do not add salt to the sponge, as this would inhibit the yeast.)

2 Cover with a damp dish towel and leave in a warm place. The sponge will double or triple in bulk and then fall back, which indicates it is ready to use (after about 5–6 hours).

3 The sponge starter is now ready to be mixed into a dough with the remaining flour and any other ingredients, such as butter, as directed in the recipe.

MAKING AN ITALIAN STARTER (*BIGA*)

If you wish to make an Italian *biga* for Pugliese or a similar Italian country bread, use 1½ cups unbleached plain flour. Cream the yeast with 6 tablespoons lukewarm water, then pour it into a well in the center of the flour. Gradually mix in the surrounding flour to form a firm dough. The dough should be kneaded for a few minutes and then left, covered with lightly oiled plastic wrap for 12–15 hours.

MAKING A FRENCH SOURDOUGH STARTER (*CHEF*)

It is not difficult to make a sourdough starter. The starter can be kept in the refrigerator for up to 10 days, but for longer than that it should be frozen. Bring the starter to room temperature before adding to the next batch of bread.

1 Place 1 cup flour in a large bowl and add 5 tablespoons water. Combine, then knead for 3–4 minutes to form a dough. Cover the bowl with plastic wrap and set aside at room temperature for 2–3 days. The flour that you choose will depend on the bread you wish to make; it can be whole-wheat, white or rye, or a combination of two or three.

2 After 2–3 days, the mixture will rise and aerate slightly and turn a grayish color. A soft crust may form on top the starter and it should develop a slightly sweet-sour smell.

3 Remove any crust that has formed on top of the starter and discard. Stir in ½ cup lukewarm water to make a paste and then add 1½ cups flour. The flour can be whole-wheat or a mixture of whole-wheat and white. Combine to make a dough, then transfer to a work surface and knead lightly until firm.

SOURDOUGH

The actual word "sourdough" is thought to have come from America as this style of bread was commonly made by pioneers and the word was sometimes used to describe old "Forty-Niners". However bread made by the sourdough method dates back long before the 19th century. Many traditional European rye breads are based on this method, particularly in Germany and Scandinavia where the sour flavor of the leaven complements the flavor of the rye.

In Britain sourdoughs are sometimes called acids or acid breads. Some restaurants and home bread makers have their own favorite acid breads, but generally there is not much of a tradition of sourdoughs in the British Isles. Except in Ireland, where soda bread was popular, ale barm (the fermentation liquor from beer) was the most commonly used leaven for bread making until it was replaced by baker's yeast around the middle of the last century.

4 Place the ball of dough in a bowl, cover again with plastic wrap and let sit for 1–2 days at room temperature.

5 Remove and discard any crust that forms. What remains—the *chef*—can now be used to make a sourdough bread, such as *pain de campagne rustique*. To keep the *chef* going, save about 8 ounces of the dough each time.

6 Place the dough starter in a crock or bowl, cover and keep in the fridge for up to 10 days or freeze.

MIXING, KNEADING AND RISING

The sequence and method of adding ingredients to make your dough is surprisingly important. For some breads, fresh or dried yeast is dissolved in lukewarm water and then stirred into the flour; if quick-rise dried yeast or fast-action dried yeast is used, this is added directly to the flour with warm water or milk added afterward. Read your recipe carefully before starting and warm your bowls if they are in the least bit chilly, so that the yeast gets off to a good start.

MIXING

The easiest way to mix the dough is with your hand but, if you prefer, start mixing with a spoon until the mixture is too stiff to stir, then mix by hand.

1 If using fresh or regular dried yeast, mix it with lukewarm water or milk as described in the recipe. Sift the flour, salt and any other dry ingredients (including easy-blend or fast-action dried yeast, if using) into a large, warm mixing bowl.

2 If using butter or lard, rub it in. Make a well in the center of the flour mixture and pour in the yeast mixture with the remaining lukewarm water. If oil is being used, add it now.

3 Mix the liquid into the flour using your hand, stirring in a smooth, wide motion so that all the dry ingredients are evenly incorporated and the mixture forms a dough. Knead lightly in the bowl.

KNEADING

Kneading is something you just cannot skip in bread making. If you do not have strong wrists, or simply do not enjoy it, you will have to resort to using the food processor, which takes all the effort—and much of the time—out of kneading. Better still though, learn to love it.

Kneading dough, whether by hand or machine, is the only way of warming and stretching the gluten in the flour. As the strands of gluten warm and become more elastic, so the dough becomes more springy. It is the elasticity of the dough, combined with the action of the yeast, that gives bread its light, springy texture. Insufficient kneading means that the dough cannot hold the little pockets of air, and the bread will collapse in the oven, leaving a heavy and dense loaf.

HOW TO KNEAD BY HAND

1 Place the mixed dough on a floured surface and flour your hands generously.

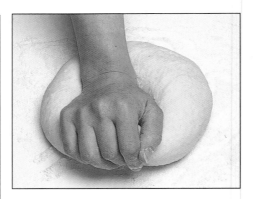

2 Press the heel of your hand firmly into the center of the dough, then curl your fingers around the edge of the dough.

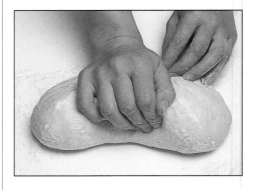

3 Pull and stretch the dough toward you and press down again, giving the dough a quarter turn as you do so.

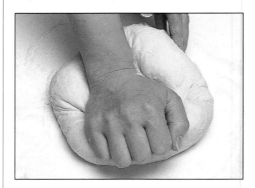

4 Continue pressing and stretching the dough, making quarter turns so that it is evenly kneaded. After about 10 minutes the dough should be supple and elastic; however, some breads need more kneading, so do check the recipe.

ADDING EXTRA INGREDIENTS

Ingredients, such as olives, can be added after kneading or they can be kneaded in after the first rising.

KNEADING IN A FOOD PROCESSOR

Unless you have an industrial-size machine, it is likely that your food processor will only be able to knead moderate amounts of dough. Don't attempt to knead more dough than recommended by the manufacturer, as it may damage the motor. If necessary, knead in small batches and then knead the dough balls together by hand afterward.

Fit the dough blade into the processor and then blend together all the dry ingredients. Add the yeast mixture, and extra lukewarm liquid and butter or oil, if required; process until the mixture comes together. Knead for 60 seconds or according to the manufacturer's instructions, then knead by hand on a floured board for 1–2 minutes.

KNEADING IN A FOOD MIXER

Check the manufacturer's instructions to make sure bread dough can be kneaded in your machine.

Combine the dry ingredients. Add the yeast, liquid and oil or butter, if using, and mix slowly, using the dough hook. The dough will tumble and fall to begin with, and then it will slowly come together. Continue kneading the dough for 3–4 minutes or according to the manufacturer's instructions.

RISING

This is the easy part of bread making—all you need now is to give the dough the right conditions, and nature and chemistry will do the rest. While kneading works and conditions the gluten in the flour, during rising (proving) the yeast does the work. The fermentation process creates carbon dioxide, which is trapped in the dough by the elastic gluten. This process also has the effect of conditioning the flour, improving the flavor and texture of the eventual loaf.

The number of times you let your bread rise will depend on the yeast you are using and the recipe. A quick-rise yeast needs no first rising, but dough using fresh yeast and other dried yeasts normally requires two risings, with some recipes calling for even more.

TEMPERATURE AND TIME

For most recipes, dough is left to rise at a temperature of about 75°–80°F, the equivalent of an airing cupboard or near a warm oven. At a cooler temperature the bread rises more slowly and some of the best-flavored breads, including baguettes, use a slower rising, giving the enzymes and starches in the flour more time to mature. The quantity of yeast used will also determine the time required for rising. More yeast means quicker rising.

1 Place the kneaded dough in a bowl that has been lightly greased. This will prevent the dough from sticking. Cover the bowl with a damp dish towel or a piece of oiled plastic wrap to prevent a skin from forming on top.

2 Let rise until the dough has doubled in bulk. At room temperature, this should take 1½–2 hours—less if the temperature is warmer; more if the room is cool. It can even be left to rise in the refrigerator for about 8 hours.

A FEW SIMPLE RULES

◆ Warm bowls and other equipment.

◆ Use the correct amount of yeast: too much will speed up the rising process but will spoil the flavor and will mean the loaf stales more quickly.

◆ If you have a thermometer, check the temperature of the lukewarm liquid, at least until you can gauge it accurately yourself. It should be between 98°–108°F. Mixing two parts cold water with one part boiling water gives you water at roughly the right temperature.

◆ The amount of liquid required for a dough depends on several factors— type of flour, other ingredients, even the room temperature. Recipes therefore often give approximate quantities of liquid. You will soon learn to judge the ideal consistency of a dough.

◆ Do not skimp on kneading. Kneading is essential for stretching the gluten to give a well-risen, light-textured loaf.

◆ Avoid leaving dough to rise in a draught and make sure the ambient temperature is not too high, or the dough will begin to cook.

◆ Always cover the bowl during rising as a crust will form on top of the dough if the air gets to it. Plastic wrap can be pressed on to the dough itself or can be stretched over the bowl. Either way, oil the plastic wrap first or the dough will stick to it as it rises.

◆ Remember: the slower the rising, the better the taste of the bread.

PUNCHING DOWN, SHAPING AND FINAL RISING

After all the effort by the yeast to create a risen dough, it seems a shame to punch down. However, this is important, as you need to redistribute the gases in the dough that were created by fermentation. Punching down also reinvigorates the yeast, making sure that it is evenly distributed, and ensures that the bread has an even texture. It should take only a few minutes and the bread is then ready for shaping. The dough is fully risen when it has doubled in bulk. If you are not sure that it is ready, test by gently inserting a finger into the center of the dough. The dough should not immediately spring back. If it does, let sit for a little longer.

1 Punch down the risen dough using your knuckles. The British call this "knocking back the dough," which is an accurate description of the process. Having punched down the dough, place it on a floured work surface and knead lightly for 1–2 minutes.

SHAPING
There are several ways of shaping the dough to fit in a loaf pan.

1 The easiest way is to shape the dough roughly into an oval and place it in the pan, with the smooth side on top.

2 Alternatively, roll out the dough into a rectangle, a little longer than the pan. Roll it up like a Swiss roll, tuck in the ends and place the roll in the pan, with the seam-side down.

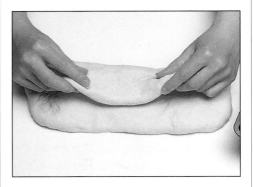

3 Another method for shaping the dough is to roll it out into a rectangle and fold it in half lengthwise, pinching the edges together on the sides and flattening the dough out slightly with the heel of your hand. Fold the dough over once more to make a double thickness and pinch the edges together again. Now gently roll the dough backward and forward until it has a well-rounded shape.

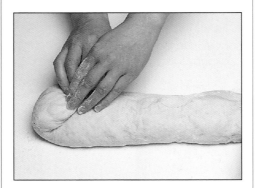

4 Fold in the two short ends and place the dough in the prepared pan with the seam along the bottom.

SHAPING A COB LOAF

1 Shape the dough into a round and then press along the center with your hand. Turn the dough over, so that the smooth side is on top.

2 Shape the dough into a round or oval and place it on a baking sheet.

TIPS
◆ Always punch down the dough after the first rising and knead lightly to redistribute the yeast and the gases formed by fermentation, otherwise you may end up with large holes in the loaf or the crust may lift up and become detached from the crumb.
◆ Rising the dough in a warm place is not always necessary—it is simply a method of speeding up the process. Dough will rise (albeit very slowly) even in the refrigerator. However, wherever you decide to rise your dough the temperature must be constant. Avoid drafts or hot spots, as both will spoil the bread and may cause it to bake unevenly.
◆ Some breads may need slashing either before final rising or during this period (see next section).

SHAPING A BAGUETTE

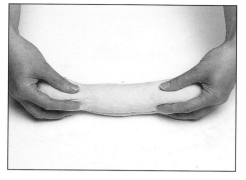

1 Divide the dough into equal pieces. Shape each piece into a ball and then into a rectangle measuring 6 × 3 inches. Fold the bottom third up and the top third down lengthwise. Press the edges together to seal them. Repeat twice, then stretch each piece to a 13–14-inch loaf.

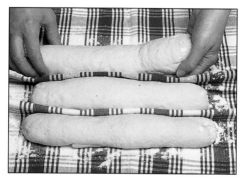

2 Place within the folds of a pleated, floured dish towel or in *bannetons*.

SHAPING A BRAID

1 Divide the dough into three equal pieces. Roll each piece into a 10-inch "sausage" about 1½ inches thick.

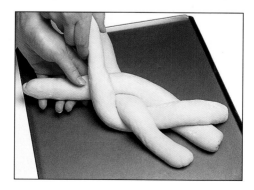

2 Place the three "sausages" on a greased baking sheet. Either start the braid in the center, braiding each end in turn, or pinch the pieces firmly together at one end, then braid.

3 When you have finished, pinch the ends together, and turn them under.

FINAL RISING

After shaping the dough and placing it on the baking sheet or in the pan, there is usually a final rising before baking. Depending on the warmth of the room, this can take ¾–1½ hours, although in a very cool room it may take up to 4 hours. Cover the dough so that the surface does not crust over. Oiled plastic wrap placed over the pan or directly on the bread is the best method. The timing is important as over-rising means the loaf may collapse in the oven, while too little proving will mean the loaf will be heavy and flat.

BELOW: A loaf ready for the final rising.

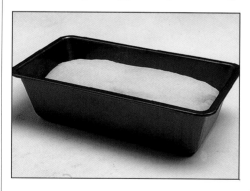

BELOW: After rising the dough should be doubled in size—no more.

PROVING BASKETS

Professional bakers use proving baskets called *bannetons* for baguettes, and circular *couronnes* for round loaves. Some are lined with linen. Proving baskets are available at good kitchenware shops but, depending on the shape you require, you can improvise with baskets and/or earthenware dishes. Simply dust a linen dish towel liberally with flour and use to line the container.

BELOW: A proving basket will give your loaves a professional finish.

CHOOSING PANS

Choosing the right size loaf pan can be a tricky business. If it is too small, the dough will spill over the top. If it is too large, the final loaf will be badly shaped and uneven. As a general rule the pan should be about twice the size of the dough. Professional bakers use black pans, which are considered to be better than shiny metal ones, as they absorb the heat better, giving a crisper crust. Always warm a pan before using and then grease it with melted lard, vegetable oil or unsalted butter. Experiment to see what you find most successful. Baking sheets should also be greased or buttered to prevent sticking.

ABOVE: Sesame seeds

ABOVE: Wheat germ

ABOVE: Sunflower seeds

ABOVE: Caraway seeds

loaf and San Francisco sourdough bread have no toppings as such, but a dusting of flour gives an attractive matte sheen to the finished loaf.

Grated cheese and sautéed onions also make more substantial as well as tasty and attractive toppings and many Italian breads demonstrate a rich variety of toppings—whole green or black olives, chunks of sun-dried tomatoes and roasted bell peppers are frequently added to ciabattas and focaccias. As with glazes, toppings can also be added during and sometimes after cooking. Small breads, such as Vienna rolls, are baked until just golden, brushed with milk or cream and then sprinkled with sea salt, cumin or caraway seeds. They are then returned to the oven for a few more moments until cooked.

BELOW: For a dinner party or a buffet, bake a batch of rolls with assorted toppings.

BAKING TIMES

This will depend on the recipe, the size of the loaf and the heat of the oven. As a general rule, rolls take about 20 minutes, round country breads 40–50 minutes and pan loaves a little longer, 45–60 minutes. To check if bread is ready, remove it from the oven and tap firmly on the base of the loaf with your knuckles. It should have a hollow sound. If it seems soft or does not sound hollow, bake for a little longer.

ABOVE: Check that rolls are ready by gently turning one over in a clean dish towel. The underside should be firm and golden, with no trace of moisture.

ABOVE: To check that a loaf is cooked, tap the base with your knuckles. It should be firm and sound hollow.

ADDING MOISTURE TO THE OVEN

A baker's oven is completely sealed and therefore produces the necessary steam for an evenly risen loaf. At home, glazing helps to produce steam, as does a pan of boiling water placed in the bottom of the oven, or you can spray water into the oven two or three times during cooking.

WHAT WENT WRONG

DOUGH WON'T RISE

You may have forgotten the yeast or the yeast may be past its "use-by" date and is dead. To save the dough, make up another batch, making certain the yeast is active. This dough can then be kneaded into the original dough. Alternatively, dissolve the new yeast in warm water and work it into the dough. Another time, always check that yeast is active before adding to flour.

SIDES AND BOTTOM OF BREAD ARE TOO PALE

The oven temperature was too low, or the pan did not allow heat to penetrate the crust. To remedy this, turn the loaf out of its pan and return it to the oven, placing it upside-down on a shelf, for 5–10 minutes.

CRUST TOO SOFT

There was insufficient steam in the oven. You could glaze the crusts before baking next time and spray the inside of the oven with water. Alternatively, place a little hot water in an ovenproof dish in the bottom of the oven during baking. This problem particularly besets French breads and other crusty loaves, which require a certain amount of steam in the oven.

CRUST TOO HARD

Using too much glaze or having too much steam in the oven can harden the crust, so use less glaze next time. To soften a crusty loaf, leave it overnight in a plastic bag.

CRUST SEPARATES FROM THE BREAD

This is caused either by the dough drying out during rising, or by the oven temperature being too low and the dough expanding unevenly. Next time, cover the dough with plastic wrap or waxed paper to prevent any moisture loss while rising, and ensure that the oven is preheated to the correct temperature, so that heat penetrates uniformly throughout the loaf.

SOFT PALE CRUST

This could be because the bread was not baked for long enough or perhaps the oven temperature was too low. When you think bread is ready, tap it firmly underneath; it should sound hollow. If it does not, return the bread to the oven, only this time placing it directly on the oven shelf.

LOAF IS CRUMBLY AND DRY

Either the bread was baked for too long or you used too much flour. Next time check the quantities in the recipe. It is also possible that the oven was too hot. Next time reduce the temperature and check the loaf when the crust looks golden brown.

LARGE HOLES IN LOAF

Either the dough was not punched down properly before shaping or it was not kneaded enough originally.

BREAD HAS A YEASTY FLAVOR

Too much yeast was used. If doubling recipe quantities, do not double the amount of yeast but use one and a half times the amount. In addition, do not overcompensate for a cool room by adding extra yeast unless you don't mind a yeasty flavor. Wait a little longer instead—the bread will rise in the end.

LOAF COLLAPSES IN THE OVEN

Either the wrong flour was used for a particular recipe or the dough was left too long for the second rising and has over-risen. As a rule, the dough should only double in bulk.

LOAF IS DENSE AND FLAT

Too much liquid was used and the dough has become too soft, or was not kneaded enough. Check the recipe for quantities of liquid needed until you are confident about judging the consistency of the dough. The dough should be kneaded firmly for at least 10 minutes.

BREAD-MAKING MACHINES

Bread machines may take the fun out of bread making, but if you enjoy home-made bread on a daily basis, they make it an incredibly easy process. All you need to do is add the correct ingredients, press the right buttons and—presto—a few hours later, you have a freshly cooked loaf of bread!

Many bread makers have a timer switch, so that you can program your bread to be ready when you get up in the morning. Almost all bread machines will make a variety of different types and sizes of loaves, and many have a feature where the bread machine does the kneading and rising, leaving the baking up to you—useful for French loaves, pizzas or any other breads that are not a standard loaf shape.

THINGS TO LOOK OUT FOR WHEN BUYING A BREAD-MAKING MACHINE

◆ Unless you are likely to need only one small loaf a day, choose a machine with the option of making small, medium and large loaves.

◆ "Rapid-bake": this cuts down on resting time, and by recommending extra yeast, also cuts down on rising. You will get a loaf in under 2 hours.

◆ Dough (or manual) cycle: allows you to remove the dough prior to shaping when making loaves that are not the standard "loaf" shape.

◆ Crust color: some bread makers have the option of a dark, medium or pale crust.

◆ Sweet bread cycle: breads that are high in sugar or fat need to bake at slightly lower temperatures, otherwise these ingredients tend to burn. A sweet bread cycle means that the bread-making machine will automatically adjust the heat to allow for this, if programmed to do so first.

◆ Timer feature: this useful feature allows you to set the bread maker so that the bread is ready for when you get up in the morning or when the children come home from school.

USING A BREAD MACHINE

1 Add the easy-blend or fast-action yeast to the bread pan. If you are making a quick or rapid-bake loaf, you may need to add up to one-and-a-half times the usual quantity of yeast, but check the manufacturer's instructions.

2 Add the remaining ingredients to the bread pan and place in the machine. Select the type of loaf you wish to bake, the size and color of the crust.

3 Dried fruit, olives or other ingredients used to flavor breads are added after the initial kneading. This is to ensure that they are not broken up too much. Depending on the type of loaf you chose to make, your bread will be ready to eat in 2–5 hours.

TIPS FOR CONVERTING RECIPES

Once you're familiar with your bread machine and confident using suggested recipes, you will probably want to adapt some of your own favorite recipes. A loaf baked in a bread-making machine will, of course, always be "loaf-shaped," but since most bread makers have a dough cycle (where the dough is kneaded but not baked), it is possible to prepare rolls, ciabatta and baguettes—indeed most breads featured in this book. It is important that you reduce the recipe according to the maximum capacity of your machine (and even more if you wish to make a small loaf).

Make sure that the proportions of all the essential ingredients for the recipe are approximately as follows:

FOR A 1 POUND LOAF
Flour: 2–2¾ cups
Liquid (water or milk): ¾–1 cup
Salt: ¼–1 teaspoon
Fat: 2 teaspoons–3 tablespoons
Salt: 2 teaspoons–3 tablespoons
*Dried yeast: 1½ teaspoons–
1 tablespoon*

FOR A 1½ POUND LOAF
Flour: 3–4 cups
Liquid (water or milk): 1–1¼ cups
Salt: ½–1½ teaspoons
Fat: 1–4 tablespoons
*Dried yeast: 1½ teaspoons–
1 tablespoon*

◆ If adding fruit or other ingredients, reduce the quantities proportionately.

◆ Always use a fast-action yeast.

◆ If adding eggs, remember that one large egg is roughly equal to 4 tablespoons liquid, so reduce the liquid accordingly.

◆ When adapting a recipe, monitor the machine carefully and make a note of any adjustments you may need to make. For instance, pay attention to whether the mixture is too moist or whether the machine struggles to knead the dough. If the loaf is too tall, this may be because you've added too much liquid, yeast or sugar, or added insufficient salt.

BREAD-MAKING EQUIPMENT

Bread making is not an exact science, and you do not need a fully equipped kitchen with state-of-the-art utensils if you decide to try it. In the long run, though, you may decide that some things are essential and others could be useful.

SCALES/WEIGHTS
A scale with weights is more accurate but a spring scale is easier to use and more convenient (especially if you have a tendency to lose the weights). Bear in mind, if buying a scale for bread making, you will probably be using large quantities of flours and will therefore need a large-size scale with a deep basin.

MEASURING CUPS
Heatproof glass cups are most convenient, as liquids can safely be heated in them in

BELOW: Be sure to get a scale with a large measuring bowl.

LEFT: Sieves for flour or spices

the microwave and they are dishwasher safe. Measurements should be clearly marked on the outside; be sure to buy cups with the measurements recorded clearly on the outside so that you can follow any recipe with ease.

MEASURING SPOONS
These are useful in the kitchen for adding small quantities of spices. A set of spoons measures from ¼ teaspoon to 1 tablespoon.

FOOD PROCESSOR
Most food processors can mix and knead dough extremely efficiently and in

a fraction of the time it would take by hand. Always check the instruction book about bread making since only the larger machines can handle large amounts of dough, and you may find that it is necessary to knead the dough in batches.

ELECTRIC MIXER
An electric mixer fitted with a dough hook will knead dough in a time similar to that taken to knead by hand but with much less effort. Small machines can cope with only small amounts of dough, and if you are considering buying a machine for bread-making purposes, make sure that the equipment is suitable for the quantities of bread you are likely to want to make.

SIEVES
Some finer breads may require the flour to be sifted, so it is worth having at least one large sieve for flours and a smaller sieve should you wish to add ground spices or dust the loaves with flour or confectioners' sugar after baking them.

ABOVE: A selection of glass bowls

BOWLS

If you do not have a selection already, it is worth buying some now as it is not possible to make bread (at least in the kitchen) without at least two good-sized bowls. Choose a bowl with a wide mouth, which is still deep enough to contain the batter or dough. A smaller china or glass bowl is also useful (although you can use the measuring cup) for making up dried yeast.

ROLLING PIN

Some doughs need to be rolled out and you will need a large rolling pin for this job. A wooden rolling pin that is long and smooth and has no separate handles is ideal for bread making.

DOUGH KNIFE OR SCRAPER

This is extremely handy when kneading dough by hand. The rectangular piece of steel on a wooden handle is particularly useful in the early part of kneading, for lifting and working sticky or difficult doughs. The blades normally measure about 4 × 5 inches and should ideally be slightly flexible rather than rigid.

COOK'S KNIFE

You will need a sharp knife for slashing the dough—either during rising or just before baking. Some recipe books suggest using a razor for this job but the blade does need to be very sharp indeed. Since a good cook's knife can be kept in razor-sharp condition, this is the preferable option and adds a professional touch to your loaves.

ABOVE: Bread knife and cook's knife

LEFT: Dough knife/scraper

ABOVE: Rolling pin

ABOVE: Pastry brushes

BREAD KNIFE

A dull knife can wreak havoc on a fresh loaf of bread, so make sure you use a good bread knife. Bread should be cut in a sawing motion, which is why bread knives have long serrated blades. A plain cook's knife, although it will cut through the bread, will spoil the texture of the crumb.

PASTRY BRUSH

This is essential for glazing loaves and rolls. Choose a good, wide brush. It is worth spending extra for a brush that will not lose its bristles. Use a brush made from natural fibers; nylon will melt if used for brushing hot loaves during cooking.

BREAD PANS

Bread pans come in all sizes, and it is worth having a selection. Include a 1-pound and preferably two 2¼-pound pans so that you can make loaves in a variety of shapes and sizes. If the pans are labeled with their dimensions, rather than

BELOW: Shallow loaf and cake pans

their capacity, look for 7 × 3-inch (equivalent to 1 pound) and 9 × 5-inch (equivalent to 2¼-pound). Other useful sizes are 12 × 4-inch and 10 × 4-inch. Professional bakers prefer matte black pans, which absorb the heat better than the shiny ones and therefore make the crust crisper. The wider shallow pans are

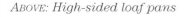

ABOVE: High-sided loaf pans

mostly used for fruit breads. Pan loaves are baked in plain, high-sided pans; farmhouse loaves are slightly shallower and pans may be stamped with the word "Farmhouse." Cake pans are sometimes used for bread making. Monkey bread, for instance, is baked in a 9-inch springform ring cake pan, while buchty—breakfast rolls that are batch-baked—require a square, loose-bottomed cake pan with straight sides that will support the rolls as they rise.

Several speciality breads are baked in a deep 6-inch cake pan. These breads include *panettone* and Sally Lunn.

If you are fond of baking focaccia, you will find a 10-inch pizza pan or shallow round cake pan invaluable.

MOLDS

There are various sizes of brioche molds for the traditional, fluted brioche, including individual bun size. A *kugelhopf* mold is a fluted ring mold essential for making the Alsace or German *kugelhopf* or the Viennese *gugelhupf*. A savarin mold is a straight-sided ring mold for

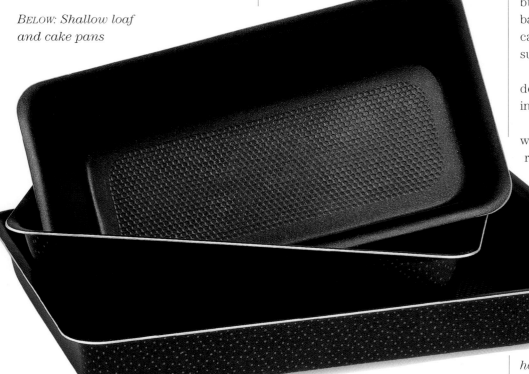

savarins and other ring-shaped breads. If you don't have the correct mold, it is sometimes possible to improvise. Boston brown bread, for instance, can be baked in a special mold, but the heatproof glass jar from a cafetière coffee maker can be used instead, or even two 1-pound coffee cans, without the lids, work perfectly well once they have been washed and dried.

BELOW: Baking sheets and patty tins

BAKING SHEETS

When buying baking sheets, look for ones that are either completely flat, or have a lip only on one long edge. This makes it easier to slide bread or rolls on to a wire rack. Strong, heavy baking sheets distribute the heat evenly.

MUFFIN PANS

Muffin pans with 3-inch cups are very useful for making elaborately shaped rolls like the aptly named New England Fantans, while larger popover pans come into their own for specialties like Georgian Khachapuri. The pans support the dough while it is filled with cheese and then tied into a topknot.

FLOWER POTS

Earthenware flower pots can also be used for baking. These need to be tempered before being used for bread. Brush the new, perfectly clean pots liberally inside and out with oil and place in a hot oven (about 400°F) for about 30 minutes. (This can conveniently be done while you are cooking something else.) Do this several times until the pots are impregnated with oil. They can then be used for baking bread and will need very little greasing.

BELOW: Earthenware flower pots make unusual molds for loaves.

LEFT: A French fluted brioche mold and a savarin or ring mold

LONGUETS
Longuets are molded pieces of steel, like corrugated iron, used for baking baguettes. They are designed with the professional baker in mind but will probably fit in an average size oven.

BAKING STONE
Baking stones are now widely available, sold principally for pizzas but also useful for making thick crusted loaves. They are the nearest thing to replicating an authentic brick-floored oven. The stones are heated in the oven and then the bread is placed on top.

BANNETONS AND COURONNES
These are the canvas-lined proving baskets used by French bakers for their bread: *bannetons* are used for baguettes, *couronnes* for round loaves. In Germany, sourdough bread is sometimes proved in a floured basket, which has the effect of creating a crust that looks like wicker.

GRIDDLE
This is a heavy cast-iron pan used on top of the stove for griddle cakes, soda farls, bannocks and even Indian breads like missi rotis and chapatis. Weight is the important feature with griddles, so that heat can be evenly dispersed.

Griddles can have handles or have the more old-fashioned design of a hooped handle over the entire pan, often with a small hoop in the center which would have been used to hang the griddle over a peat fire. In Scotland, where they are still widely used, griddles are also known as girdles.

Square-shaped griddles that come with metal hoops for English muffins and crumpets are also available at good kitchen supply stores. The hoops have a diameter of about 4 inches and are about 1-inch-deep.

BELOW: This short, deep banneton is ideal for shorter French loaves.

ABOVE: Very long bannetons are designed for supporting baguettes during the final rising.

BELOW: A griddle for pikelets and other free form breads, such as griddle-baked soda bread and oatcakes.

BREAD RECIPES OF THE WORLD

There are few things more pleasurable than the aroma and taste of freshly cooked homemade bread. This collection of recipes includes savory and sweet classics from around the world, as well as a good selection of lesser-known specialties. A wide variety of flours, all of which are readily available, has been used to create distinctive breads which reflect the different flavors of the regions. These recipes aim to take the mystery out of bread making and inspire you to try baking many different and delicious breads.

BRITISH BREADS

The range of British breads is extensive and includes a variety of shapes with picturesque names, including the bloomer, cob, split tin and cottage loaf. The textures and tastes are influenced by different ingredients and cooking methods. Welsh clay pot loaves, as their name suggests, are baked in clay flower pots and flavored with herbs and garlic, while in Scotland, where bannocks and oatcakes are cooked on a girdle or griddle, grains such as barley and oatmeal contribute to the country-fresh flavors. Doughs enriched with dried fruits, such as Welsh bara brith and Cornish saffron bread, are delicious regional specialties.

GRANARY COB

4 cups Granary or malthouse flour
2 teaspoons salt
½ ounce fresh yeast
1¼ cups lukewarm water or milk and
water mixed

FOR THE TOPPING
2 tablespoons water
½ teaspoon salt
wheat germ or cracked wheat,
to sprinkle

MAKES 1 ROUND LOAF

Cob is an old word meaning "head." If you make a slash across the top of the
dough, the finished loaf, known as a Danish cob, will look like a large roll.
A Coburg cob has a cross cut in the top before baking.

1 Lightly flour a baking sheet. Sift the flour and salt together in a large bowl and make a well in the center. Place in a very low oven for 5 minutes to warm.

2 Mix the yeast with a little of the water or milk mixture, then blend in the rest. Add the yeast mixture to the center of the flour and mix to a dough.

3 Turn out onto a lightly floured surface and knead for about 10 minutes, until smooth and elastic. Place in a lightly oiled bowl, cover with lightly oiled plastic wrap and let rise, in a warm place, for 1¼ hours or until doubled in bulk.

4 Turn the dough out onto a lightly floured surface and punch down. Knead for 2–3 minutes, then roll into a ball, making sure the dough looks like a plump round cushion, otherwise it will become too flat. Place in the center of the prepared baking sheet. Cover with an inverted bowl and let rise, in a warm place, for 30–45 minutes.

5 Mix the water and salt and brush over the bread. Sprinkle with wheat germ or cracked wheat.

6 Meanwhile, preheat the oven to 450°F. Bake for 15 minutes, then reduce the oven temperature to 400°F and bake for another 20 minutes or until the loaf is firm to the touch and sounds hollow when tapped on the bottom. Cool on a wire rack.

CHEESE AND ONION LOAF

Almost a meal in itself, this hearty bread tastes delicious as an accompaniment to salads and cold meats or with soup.

1 Lightly grease a 10 × 4-inch loaf pan. Melt 2 tablespoons of the butter in a heavy frying pan and sauté the onion until it is soft and light golden. Set aside to cool.

2 Sift the flour into a large bowl and stir in the yeast, mustard, salt and pepper. Stir in three-quarters of the grated cheese and the onion. Make a well in the center. Add the milk and water; blend to a soft dough. Turn out onto a lightly floured surface and knead for 10 minutes, until smooth and elastic.

3 Place the dough in a lightly oiled bowl, cover with lightly oiled plastic wrap and let rise, in a warm place, for 45–60 minutes or until doubled in bulk.

4 Turn the dough out onto a lightly floured surface, punch down, and knead gently. Divide into 20 equal pieces and shape into small rounds. Place half in the prepared pan and brush with some melted butter. Top with the remaining rounds of dough and brush with the remaining butter.

5 Cover with oiled plastic wrap and let rise for 45 minutes, until the dough reaches the top of the pan. Meanwhile, preheat the oven to 375°F.

6 Sprinkle the remaining cheese on the top. Bake for 40–45 minutes or until risen and golden brown. Cool on a wire rack.

1 onion, finely chopped
3½ tablespoons butter
4 cups unbleached white bread flour
¼ ounce envelope easy-blend dried yeast
1 teaspoon mustard powder
1½ cups grated aged cheddar cheese
⅔ cup lukewarm milk
⅔ cup lukewarm water
salt and ground black pepper

MAKES 1 LARGE LOAF

COOK'S TIP
If you prefer, use ¾ ounce fresh yeast instead of the easy-blend yeast. Mix the fresh yeast with the milk until dissolved, then add to the flour.

POPPY-SEEDED BLOOMER

6 cups unbleached white bread flour
2 teaspoons salt
½ ounce fresh yeast
1⅞ cups water

FOR THE TOPPING
½ teaspoon salt
2 tablespoons water
poppy seeds, for sprinkling

MAKES 1 LARGE LOAF

This satisfying white bread, which is the British version of the chunky baton loaf found throughout Europe, is made by a slower rising method and with less yeast than usual. It produces a longer-keeping loaf with a fuller flavor. The dough takes about 8 hours to rise, so you'll need to start this bread early in the morning.

1 Lightly grease a baking sheet. Sift the flour and salt together into a large bowl and make a well in the center.

2 Mix the yeast and ⅔ cup of the water in a cup or bowl. Mix in the remaining water. Add to the center of the flour. Mix, gradually incorporating the surrounding flour, until the mixture forms a firm dough.

3 Turn out onto a lightly floured surface and knead the dough very well, for at least 10 minutes, until smooth and elastic. Place the dough in a lightly oiled bowl, cover with lightly oiled plastic wrap and let rise, at cool room temperature, about 60–65°F, for 5–6 hours or until doubled in bulk.

4 Punch down the dough, turn out onto a lightly floured surface and knead it thoroughly for about 5 minutes. Return the dough to the bowl, and re-cover. Let rise, at room temperature, for another 2 hours or slightly longer.

6 Place it seam side up on a lightly floured baking sheet, cover and let rest for 15 minutes. Turn the loaf over and place on the greased baking sheet. Plump up by tucking the dough under the sides and ends. Using a sharp knife, cut 6 diagonal slashes on the top.

7 Let rest, covered, in a warm place, for 10 minutes. Meanwhile, preheat the oven to 450°F.

8 Combine the salt and water and brush this glaze over the bread. Sprinkle with poppy seeds.

9 Spray the oven with water, bake the bread for 20 minutes, then reduce the oven temperature to 400°F; bake for 25 more minutes, or until golden. Transfer to a wire rack to cool.

COOK'S TIP
The traditional cracked, crusty appearance of this loaf is difficult to achieve in a domestic oven. However, you can get a similar result by spraying the oven with water before baking. If the underneath of the loaf is not very crusty at the end of baking, turn the loaf over on the baking sheet, switch off the heat and leave in the oven for another 5–10 minutes.

VARIATION
For a more rustic loaf, replace up to half the flour with whole-wheat bread flour.

5 Punch down again and repeat the thorough kneading. Let the dough rest for 5 minutes, then roll out on a lightly floured surface into a rectangle 1-inch thick. Roll the dough up from one long side and shape it into a square-ended thick baton shape about 13 × 5 inches.

COTTAGE LOAF

6 cups unbleached white bread flour
2 teaspoons salt
¾ ounce fresh yeast
1⅔ cups lukewarm water

MAKES 1 LARGE ROUND LOAF

Snipping the top and bottom sections of the dough at 2-inch intervals not only looks good but also helps the loaf to expand in the oven.

COOK'S TIPS
• To ensure a good-shaped cottage loaf the dough needs to be firm enough to support the weight of the top ball.
• Do not over-proof the dough on the second rising or the loaf may topple over—but even if it does it will still taste good.

1 Lightly grease 2 baking sheets. Sift the flour and salt together into a large bowl and make a well in the center.

2 Mix the yeast in ⅔ cup of the water until dissolved. Pour into the center of the flour with the remaining water and mix to a firm dough.

3 Knead on a lightly floured surface for 10 minutes until smooth and elastic. Place in a lightly oiled bowl, cover with lightly oiled plastic wrap and let rise, in a warm place, for about 1 hour or until doubled in bulk.

4 Turn out onto a lightly floured surface and punch down. Knead for 2–3 minutes, then divide the dough into two-thirds and one-third; shape each part into a ball.

5 Place the balls of dough on the prepared baking sheets. Cover with inverted bowls and let rise, in a warm place, for about 30 minutes (see Cook's Tips).

6 Gently flatten the top of the larger round of dough and, with a sharp knife, cut a cross in the center, 1½ inches across. Brush with a little water and place the smaller round on top.

7 Carefully press a hole through the middle of the top ball, down into the lower part, using your thumb and first two fingers of one hand. Cover with lightly oiled plastic wrap and let rest in a warm place for about 10 minutes. Preheat the oven to 425°F, and place the bread on the lower shelf. It will finish expanding as the oven heats up. Bake for 35–40 minutes or until golden brown and sounding hollow when tapped. Cool on a wire rack.

WELSH CLAY POT LOAVES

These breads are flavored with chives, sage, parsley and garlic. You can use any selection of your favorite herbs. For even more flavor, try adding a little grated raw onion and grated cheese to the dough.

1 cup whole-wheat bread flour
3 cups unbleached white bread flour
1½ teaspoons salt
½ ounce fresh yeast
⅔ cup lukewarm milk
1½ cups lukewarm water
4 tablespoons butter, melted
1 tablespoon chopped fresh chives
1 tablespoon chopped fresh parsley
1 teaspoon chopped fresh sage
1 garlic clove, crushed
beaten egg, for glazing
fennel seeds, for sprinkling (optional)

MAKES 2 LOAVES

COOK'S TIP
To prepare and seal new clay flower pots, clean them thoroughly, oil them inside and outside and bake them three or four times. Preheat the oven to about 400°F and bake for 30–40 minutes. Try to do this while you are baking other foods.

4 Turn the dough out onto a lightly floured surface and punch down. Divide in half. Shape and fit into the prepared flower pots. They should about half fill the pots. Cover with oiled plastic wrap and let rise for 30–45 minutes, in a warm place, or until the dough is 1 inch from the tops of the pots.

5 Meanwhile, preheat the oven to 400°F. Brush the tops with beaten egg and sprinkle with fennel seeds, if using. Bake for 35–40 minutes or until golden. Turn out onto a wire rack to cool.

1 Lightly grease 2 clean 5½-inch diameter, 4½-inch high clay flowerpots. Sift the flours and salt together into a large bowl and make a well in the center. Blend the yeast with a little of the milk until smooth, then stir in the remaining milk. Pour the yeast liquid into the center of the flour and sprinkle over a little of the flour from around the edge. Cover the bowl and let sit in a warm place for 15 minutes.

2 Add the water, melted butter, herbs and garlic to the flour mixture and blend to form a dough. Turn out onto a lightly floured surface and knead for about 10 minutes, until the dough is smooth and elastic.

3 Place in a lightly oiled bowl, cover with lightly oiled plastic wrap and let rise, in a warm place, for 1¼–1½ hours or until doubled in bulk.

SPLIT PAN

5 cups unbleached white bread flour,
plus extra for dusting
2 teaspoons salt
½ ounce fresh yeast
1¼ cups lukewarm water
4 tablespoons lukewarm milk

MAKES 1 LOAF

As its name suggests, this homey loaf is so called because of the center split.
Some bakers mold the dough in two loaves—they join together while proving
but retain the characteristic crack after baking.

1 Lightly grease a 2-pound loaf pan (7¼ × 4½ inches). Sift the flour and salt together into a large bowl and make a well in the center. Mix the yeast with half the lukewarm water in a bowl, then stir in the remaining water.

2 Pour the yeast mixture into the center of the flour and, using your fingers, mix in a little flour. Gradually mix in more of the flour from around the edge of the bowl to form a thick, smooth batter.

3 Sprinkle a little more flour from around the edge over the batter and leave in a warm place to "sponge." Bubbles will appear in the batter after about 20 minutes. Add the milk and remaining flour; mix to a firm dough.

4 Place on a lightly floured surface and knead for about 10 minutes, until smooth and elastic. Place in a lightly oiled bowl, cover with lightly oiled plastic wrap and let rise, in a warm place, for 1–1¼ hours or until nearly doubled in bulk.

5 Punch down the dough and turn out onto a lightly floured surface. Shape it into a rectangle, the length of the pan. Roll up lengthwise, tuck the ends under and place seam side down in the prepared pan. Cover and let rise, in a warm place, for about 20–30 minutes, or until nearly doubled in bulk.

6 Using a sharp knife, make one deep central slash the length of the bread; dust with flour. Let sit for 10–15 minutes.

7 Meanwhile, preheat the oven to 450°F. Bake for 15 minutes, then reduce the oven temperature to 400°F. Bake for 20–25 more minutes or until the bread is golden and sounds hollow when tapped on the bottom. Turn out onto a wire rack to cool.

SHAPED DINNER ROLLS

These professional-looking rolls are perfect for entertaining. You can always make double the amount of dough and freeze half, tightly wrapped. Just thaw, glaze and bake as required.

4 cups unbleached white bread flour
2 teaspoons salt
½ teaspoon sugar
¼ ounce envelope
easy-blend dried yeast
¼ cup butter or margarine
1 cup lukewarm milk
1 egg

FOR THE TOPPING
1 egg yolk
1 tablespoon water
poppy seeds and sesame seeds,
for sprinkling

MAKES 12 ROLLS

1 Lightly grease 2 baking sheets. Sift the flour and salt together into a large bowl and stir in the sugar and yeast. Add the butter or margarine and rub in until the mixture resembles fine bread crumbs.

3 Turn the dough out onto a lightly floured surface, punch down and knead for 2–3 minutes. Divide the dough into 12 equal pieces and shape into rolls as described in steps 4–8.

5 *To make trefoils:* Divide each piece of dough into three and roll into balls. Place the three balls together in a triangular shape.

6 *To make batons:* Shape each piece of dough into an oblong and slash the surface of each with diagonal cuts just before baking.

7 *To make cottage rolls:* Divide each piece of dough into two-thirds and one-third and shape into rounds. Place the small one on top of the large one and make a hole through the center with the handle of a wooden spoon.

8 *To make knots:* Shape each piece of dough into a long roll and tie a single knot, pulling the ends through.

2 Make a well in the center. Add the milk and egg to the well and mix to a dough. Knead on a lightly floured surface for 10 minutes until smooth and elastic. Place in a lightly oiled bowl, cover with lightly oiled plastic wrap and let rise, in a warm place, for 1 hour, or until doubled in bulk.

4 *To make braids:* divide each piece of dough into three equal pieces. Working on a lightly floured surface, roll each piece to a sausage, keeping the lengths and widths even. Pinch 3 strips together at one end, then braid them neatly but not too tightly. Pinch the ends together and tuck under the braid.

9 Place the dinner rolls on the prepared baking sheets, spacing them well apart, cover the rolls with oiled plastic wrap and let rise, in a warm place, for about 30 minutes or until doubled in bulk.

10 Meanwhile, preheat the oven to 425°F. Mix the egg yolk and water together for the glaze and brush over the rolls. Sprinkle some with poppy seeds and some with sesame seeds. Bake for 15–18 minutes or until golden. Lift the rolls off the sheet using a spatula and transfer to a wire rack to cool.

CRUMPETS

Homemade crumpets are less doughy and not as heavy as most supermarket versions. Serve them lightly toasted, oozing with butter.

2 cups all-purpose flour
2 cups white bread flour
2 teaspoon salt
2½ cups milk and water mixed
2 tablespoons sunflower oil
1 tablespoon sugar
½ ounce fresh yeast
½ teaspoon baking soda
½ cup lukewarm water

MAKES ABOUT 20 CRUMPETS

1 Lightly grease a griddle or heavy frying pan and 4 × 3¼-inch plain cookie cutters or crumpet rings.

2 Sift the flours and salt together into a large bowl and make a well in the center. Heat the milk and water mixture, oil and sugar until lukewarm. Mix the yeast with ⅔ cup of this liquid.

3 Add the yeast mixture and remaining liquid to the center of the flour and beat vigorously for about 5 minutes, until smooth and elastic. Cover with lightly oiled plastic wrap and let rise, in a warm place, for about 1½ hours, or until the mixture is bubbly and about to fall.

4 Dissolve the soda in the lukewarm water and stir into the batter. Re-cover and let rise for 30 minutes.

5 Place the cutters or crumpet rings on the griddle and warm over medium heat. Fill the cutters or rings a generous ½-inch deep. Cook over low heat for 6–7 minutes. The tops should be dry, with a mass of tiny holes.

6 Carefully remove the cutters or rings and turn the crumpets over. Cook for 1–2 minutes or until pale golden. Repeat with remaining batter. Serve warm.

COOK'S TIP
If the batter does not produce the characteristic bubbles, add a little more water before cooking the next batch of crumpets.

ENGLISH MUFFINS

Perfect served warm, split open and buttered for afternoon tea; or try these favorites toasted, split and topped with ham and eggs for brunch.

4 cups white bread flour
1½ teaspoons salt
1½–1⅔ cups lukewarm milk
½ teaspoon sugar
½ ounce fresh yeast
1 tablespoon melted butter or olive oil
rice flour or semolina, for dusting

MAKES 9 MUFFINS

1 Generously flour a non-stick baking sheet. Very lightly grease a griddle. Sift the flour and salt together into a large bowl and make a well in the center. Blend ⅔ cup of the milk, sugar and yeast together. Stir in the remaining milk and butter or oil.

2 Add the yeast mixture to the center of the flour and beat for 4–5 minutes, until smooth and elastic. The dough will be soft but just hold its shape. Cover with lightly oiled plastic wrap and let rise, in a warm place, for 45–60 minutes or until doubled in bulk.

3 Turn out the dough onto a well floured surface and knock back. Roll out to about ½-inch thick. Using a floured 3-inch plain cutter, cut out 9 rounds.

4 Dust with rice flour or semolina and place on the prepared baking sheet. Cover and let to rise, in a warm place, for about 20–30 minutes.

5 Warm the griddle over medium heat. Carefully transfer the muffins in batches to the griddle. Cook slowly for about 7 minutes on each side or until golden brown. Transfer to a wire rack to cool.

COOK'S TIPS
• Muffins should be cut around the outer edge only using a sharp knife and then torn apart. If toasting, toast the whole muffins first and then split them in half.
• If you'd like to serve the muffins warm, transfer them to a wire rack to cool slightly before serving.

LARDY CAKE

4 cups white bread flour
1 teaspoon salt
1 tablespoon lard
2 tablespoons sugar
¾ ounce fresh yeast
1¼ cups lukewarm water

FOR THE FILLING
6 tablespoons lard
6 tablespoons light
brown sugar
½ cup currants, slightly warmed
½ cup golden raisins,
slightly warmed
3 tablespoons mixed chopped peel
1 teaspoon allspice

FOR THE GLAZE
2 teaspoons sunflower oil
1–2 tablespoons sugar

MAKES 1 LARGE LOAF

This special rich fruit bread was originally made throughout many counties of England for celebrating the harvest. Using lard rather than butter or margarine makes an authentic lardy cake.

1 Grease a 10 × 8-inch shallow roasting pan. Sift the flour and salt into a large bowl and rub in the lard. Stir in the sugar and make a well in the center.

2 In a bowl, cream the yeast with half of the water, then blend in the remainder. Add to the center of the flour and mix to a smooth dough.

3 Turn out onto a lightly floured surface and knead for about 10 minutes until smooth and elastic. Place in a lightly oiled bowl, cover with lightly oiled plastic wrap and let rise, in a warm place, for 1 hour, or until doubled in bulk.

4 Turn the dough out onto a lightly floured surface and punch down. Knead for 2–3 minutes. Roll into a rectangle about ¼-inch thick.

5 Using half the lard for the filling, cover the top two-thirds of the dough with flakes of lard. Sprinkle on half the sugar, half the dried fruits and peel and half the allspice. Fold the bottom third up and the top third down, sealing the edges with the rolling pin.

6 Turn the dough by 90 degrees. Repeat the rolling and cover with the remaining lard, fruit and peel and allspice. Fold, seal and turn as before. Roll out the dough to fit the prepared pan. Cover with lightly oiled plastic wrap and let rise, in a warm place, for 30–45 minutes or until doubled in size.

7 Meanwhile, preheat the oven to 400°F. Brush the top of the lardy cake with sunflower oil and sprinkle with sugar.

8 Score a criss-cross pattern on top using a sharp knife, then bake for 30–40 minutes, until golden. Turn out onto a wire rack to cool slightly. Serve warm, cut into slices or squares.

CORNISH SAFFRON BREADS

Often called saffron cake, this light, delicately spiced bread contains strands of saffron and is made in a loaf pan. Whatever the name, the flavor and texture are superb.

1¼ cups milk
½ teaspoon saffron strands
3½ cups all-purpose flour
1 ounce fresh yeast
½ cup ground almonds
½ teaspoon grated nutmeg
½ teaspoon ground cinnamon
¼ cup sugar
½ teaspoon salt
6 tablespoons butter, softened
⅓ cup golden raisins
¼ cup currants

FOR THE GLAZE
2 tablespoons milk
1 tablespoon sugar

MAKES 2 LOAVES

1 Lightly grease two 2-pound loaf pans. Heat half the milk until almost boiling.

2 Place the saffron strands in a small heatproof bowl and pour in the milk. Stir gently, then set aside to infuse for 30 minutes.

3 Heat the remaining milk in the same pan until it is just lukewarm.

4 Place ½ cup flour in a small bowl, crumble in the yeast and stir in the lukewarm milk. Mix well, then let sit for about 15 minutes until the yeast starts to ferment.

5 Combine the remaining flour, ground almonds, spices, sugar and salt in a large bowl and make a well in the center. Add the saffron infusion, yeast mixture and softened butter to the center of the flour and mix to a very soft dough.

6 Turn out onto a lightly floured surface and knead for 5 minutes until smooth and elastic. Place in a lightly oiled bowl, cover with lightly oiled plastic wrap and let rise, in a warm place, for 1½–2 hours, or until doubled in bulk.

7 Turn the dough out onto a lightly floured surface, punch down, and knead in the golden raisins and currants. Divide in half and shape into two loaves. Place in the prepared pans. Cover with oiled plastic wrap and let rise, in a warm place, for 1½ hours, or until the dough reaches the top of the pans.

8 Meanwhile, preheat the oven to 425°F. Bake the loaves for 10 minutes, then reduce the oven temperature to 375°F and bake for 15–20 minutes or until golden.

9 While the loaves are baking, make the glaze. Heat the milk and sugar in a small saucepan, stirring until the sugar has dissolved. As soon as the loaves come out of the oven, brush them with the glaze, let sit in the pans for 5 minutes, then turn out onto a wire rack to cool.

BARLEY BANNOCK

1 cup barley flour
½ cup all-purpose flour or whole-
wheat flour
½ teaspoon salt
½ teaspoon cream of tartar
2 tablespoons butter or margarine
¾ cup buttermilk
½ teaspoon baking soda

MAKES 1 ROUND LOAF

*Bannocks are flat loaves about the size of a dinner plate. They are
traditionally baked on a griddle or girdle (which is the preferred name in
Scotland). Barley flour adds a wonderfully earthy flavor to the bread.*

1 Wipe the surface of a griddle with a little vegetable oil. Sift the flours, salt and cream of tartar together into a large bowl. Add the butter or margarine and rub into the flour until it resembles fine bread crumbs.

3 On a floured surface, pat the dough out to form a round about ¾-inch thick. Mark the dough into 4 wedges, using a sharp knife.

2 Combine the buttermilk and baking soda. When the mixture starts to bubble, add it to the flour. Combine to form a soft dough. Do not over-mix the dough or it will toughen.

4 Heat the griddle until hot. Cook the bannock on the griddle for 8–10 minutes per side over low heat. Do not cook too quickly or the outside will burn before the center is cooked. Cool the bannock slightly on a wire rack and eat while still warm.

COOK'S TIPS
• If you cannot locate buttermilk, then use sour milk instead. Stir 1 teaspoon lemon juice into ¾ cup milk and set aside for an hour to sour.
• If you find the earthy flavor of barley flour too strong, reduce it to ½ cup and increase the plain white flour to 1 cup. Alternatively, replace half the barley flour with fine oatmeal.

SCOTTISH OATCAKES

*1 cup medium or
fine oatmeal*
¼ teaspoon salt
pinch of baking soda
*1 tablespoon melted butter
or lard*
3–4 tablespoons hot water

MAKES 8 OATCAKES

*The crunchy texture of these tempting oatcakes makes them difficult to resist.
Serve with butter and slices of a good aged cheese.*

1 Very lightly oil a griddle or heavy frying pan. Combine the oatmeal, salt and soda in a bowl.

3 On an oatmeal-dusted surface roll each piece of dough out as thinly as possible into a round about 6 inches across and ¼ inch thick.

4 Cut each round into 4 quarters or farls. Heat the griddle over medium heat, until warm. Transfer 4 farls, using a spatula, to the griddle and cook over low heat for 4–5 minutes. The edges may start to curl.

2 Add the melted butter or lard and enough hot water to make a dough. Lightly knead on a surface dusted with oatmeal until it is smooth. Cut the dough in half.

5 Using the spatula, carefully turn the farls over and cook for 1–2 minutes. If preferred, the second side can be cooked under a preheated broiler until crisp, but not brown. Transfer to a wire rack to cool. Repeat with the remaining farls.

VARIATIONS
• Oatcakes are traditionally cooked on the griddle, but they can also be cooked in the oven at 350°F for about 20 minutes, or until pale golden in color.
• Small round oatcakes can be stamped out using a 3-inch plain cutter, if preferred.

WELSH BARA BRITH

¾ ounce fresh yeast
scant 1 cup lukewarm milk
4 cups white bread flour
6 tablespoons butter or lard
1 teaspoon allspice
½ teaspoon salt
⅓ cup light brown sugar
1 egg, lightly beaten
⅔ cup raisins, slightly warmed
scant ½ cup currants,
slightly warmed
¼ cup mixed chopped peel
1–2 tablespoons honey,
for glazing

MAKES 1 LARGE ROUND LOAF

This rich, fruity bread—the name literally means "speckled bread"—is a specialty from North Wales. The honey glaze makes a delicious topping.

1 Grease a baking sheet. In a bowl, blend the yeast with a little of the milk, then stir in the remainder. Set aside for 10 minutes.

2 Sift the flour into a large bowl and rub in the butter or lard until the mixture resembles bread crumbs. Stir in the allspice, salt and sugar and make a well in the center.

3 Add the yeast mixture and beaten egg to the center of the flour and mix into a rough dough.

4 Turn out the dough onto a lightly floured surface and knead for about 10 minutes until smooth and elastic. Place in a lightly oiled bowl, cover with lightly oiled plastic wrap and let rise, in a warm place, for 1½ hours or until doubled in bulk.

5 Turn out the dough onto a lightly floured surface, punch down, and knead in the dried fruits and peel. Shape into a round and place on the prepared baking sheet. Cover with oiled plastic wrap and let rise, in a warm place, for 1 hour or until the dough doubles in size.

6 Meanwhile, preheat the oven to 400°F. Bake for 30 minutes or until the bread sounds hollow when tapped on the bottom. If the bread starts to over-brown, cover it loosely with foil for the last 10 minutes. Transfer the bread to a wire rack, brush with honey and let cool.

VARIATIONS
• The bara brith can be baked in a 6¼–7½-cup loaf pan or deep round or square cake pan, if you prefer.
• For a more wholesome loaf, replace half the white flour with whole-wheat bread flour.

SALLY LUNN

Sally Lunn is traditionally served warm, sliced into three layers horizontally, spread with clotted cream or butter and re-assembled. It looks fantastic.

1 Lightly butter a 6-inch round cake pan, 3 inches deep. Dust lightly with flour, if the pan is not non-stick. Melt the butter in a small saucepan and then stir in the milk or cream and sugar. The mixture should be tepid. Remove from the heat, add the yeast and blend thoroughly until the yeast has dissolved. Let sit for 10 minutes or until the yeast starts to work.

2 Sift the flour and salt together into a large bowl. Stir in the lemon zest and make a well in the center. Add the yeast mixture to the center of the flour and combine to make a soft dough just stiff enough to form a shape.

3 Turn out the dough onto a lightly floured surface and knead for about 10 minutes until smooth and elastic. Shape into a ball and place in the prepared pan. Cover with lightly oiled plastic wrap and let rise, in a warm place, for 1¼–1½ hours.

4 When the dough has risen to the top of the pan, remove the plastic wrap.

5 Meanwhile, preheat the oven to 425°F. Bake for 15–20 minutes or until light golden. While the loaf is baking, heat the milk and sugar for the glaze in a small saucepan until the sugar has dissolved, then bring to a boil. Brush the glaze over the bread.

6 Let cool in the pan for 10 minutes or until the bread comes away from the side easily, then cool slightly on a wire rack before slicing and filling.

2 tablespoons butter
⅔ cup milk or
heavy cream
1 tablespoon sugar
½ ounce fresh yeast
2½ cups white bread flour
½ teaspoon salt
finely grated zest of ½ lemon

For the Glaze
1 tablespoon milk
1 tablespoon sugar

Makes 1 Round Loaf

FRENCH BREADS

Although best known for the baguette, France has many more breads to offer, from specialties like decorative wheat-ear shaped epi and kugelhopf—which introduces nuts, onion and bacon—to rustic crusty breads like pain polka and that old-fashioned rye bread, pain bouillie. Enriched doughs are popular with the French and include the rich, buttery yet light classic breakfast treats of croissants and brioche. Perfect with a cup of coffee!

CROISSANTS

Golden layers of flaky pastry, puffy, light and flavored with butter is how the best croissants should be. Serve warm on the day of baking.

3 cups white bread flour
1 cup all-purpose flour
1 teaspoon salt
2 tablespoons sugar
1/2 ounce fresh yeast
scant 1 cup lukewarm milk
1 egg, lightly beaten
1 cup butter

FOR THE GLAZE
1 egg yolk
1 tablespoon milk

MAKES 14 CROISSANTS

COOK'S TIP
Make sure that the butter and the dough are about the same temperature when combining to ensure the best results.

1 Sift the flours and salt together into a large bowl. Stir in the sugar. Make a well in the center. Mix the yeast with 3 tablespoons of the milk, then stir in the remainder. Add the yeast mixture to the center of the flour, then add the egg and gradually beat in the flour until it forms a dough.

2 Turn out onto a lightly floured surface and knead for 3–4 minutes. Place in a large lightly oiled bowl, cover with lightly oiled plastic wrap and let rise, in a warm place, for about 45 minutes–1 hour or until doubled in bulk.

3 Punch down, re-cover and chill for 1 hour. Meanwhile, flatten the butter into a block about 3/4 inch thick. Punch down the dough and turn out onto a lightly floured surface. Roll out into a rough 10-inch square, rolling the edges thinner than the center.

4 Place the block of butter diagonally in the center and fold the corners of the dough over the butter like an envelope, tucking in the edges to completely enclose the butter.

5 Roll the dough into a rectangle about 3/4-inch thick, approximately twice as long as it is wide. Fold the bottom third up and the top third down and seal the edges with a rolling pin. Wrap in plastic wrap and chill for 20 minutes.

6 Repeat the rolling, folding and chilling twice more, turning the dough by 90 degrees each time. Roll out on a floured surface into a 25 × 13-inch rectangle; trim the edges to leave a 24 × 12-inch rectangle. Cut in half lengthwise. Cut crosswise into 14 equal triangles with 6-inch bases.

7 Place the dough triangles on 2 baking sheets, cover with plastic wrap and chill for 10 minutes.

8 To shape the croissants, place each one with the wide end at the top, hold each side and pull gently to stretch the top of the triangle a little, then roll towards the point, finishing with the pointed end tucked underneath. Curve the ends toward the pointed end to make a crescent. Place on two baking sheets, spaced well apart.

9 Combine the egg yolk and milk for the glaze. Lightly brush a little glaze over the croissants, avoiding the cut edges of the dough. Cover the croissants loosely with lightly oiled plastic wrap and let rise, in a warm place, for about 30 minutes or until they are nearly doubled in size.

10 Meanwhile, preheat the oven to 425°F. Brush the croissants with the remaining glaze and bake for 15–20 minutes, or until crisp and golden. Transfer to a wire rack to cool slightly before serving warm.

VARIATION
To make chocolate-filled croissants, place a small square of semi-sweet chocolate or 1 tablespoon coarsely chopped chocolate at the wide end of each triangle before rolling up as in step 8.

PAIN BOUILLIE

This is an old-fashioned style of rye bread, made before sourdough starters were used. Rye flour is mixed with boiling water like a porridge and left overnight to ferment. The finished bread has a rich earthy flavor, with just a hint of caraway.

FOR THE PORRIDGE
2 cups rye flour
1³⁄₄ cups boiling water
1 teaspoon honey

FOR THE DOUGH
¹⁄₄ ounce fresh yeast
2 tablespoons lukewarm water
1 teaspoon caraway seeds, crushed
2 teaspoons salt
3 cups white bread flour
olive oil, for brushing

MAKES 2 LOAVES

1 Lightly grease a 9¹⁄₄ × 5-inch loaf pan. Place the rye flour for the porridge in a large bowl. Pour in the boiling water and let stand for 5 minutes. Stir in the honey. Cover with plastic wrap and let sit in a warm place for about 12 hours.

2 Make the dough. Put the yeast in a measuring cup and blend in the water. Stir the mixture into the porridge with the crushed caraway seeds and salt. Add the white flour a little at a time, mixing first with a wooden spoon and then with your hands, until the mixture forms a firm dough.

3 Turn out onto a lightly floured surface and knead for 6–8 minutes, until smooth and elastic. Return to the bowl, cover with lightly oiled plastic wrap and let rise, in a warm place, for 1¹⁄₂ hours or until doubled in bulk.

4 Turn out the dough onto a lightly floured surface and knock back. Cut into 2 equal pieces and roll each piece into a rectangle 15 × 4¹⁄₂ inches. Fold the bottom third up and the top third down and seal the edges. Turn over.

5 Brush one side of each piece of folded dough with olive oil and place side by side in the prepared pan, oiled edges next to each other. Cover with lightly oiled plastic wrap and let rise, in a warm place, for 1 hour or until the dough reaches the top of the pan.

6 Meanwhile, preheat the oven to 425°F. Brush the tops of the loaves with olive oil, and using a sharp knife, slash with one or two cuts. Bake for 30 minutes, then reduce the oven temperature to 375°F and bake for another 25–30 minutes. Turn out onto a wire rack to cool.

COOK'S TIP
Serve very thinly sliced, with a little butter, or as an accompaniment to cold meats and cheeses.

EPI

This pretty, wheat shaped crusty loaf makes a good presentation bread. The recipe uses a piece of fermented French baguette dough as a starter, which improves the flavor and texture of the finished bread.

1/4 ounce fresh yeast
generous 1 cup lukewarm water
1/2 cup 6–10-hours-old French baguette dough
2 cups white bread flour
3/4 cup all-purpose flour
1 teaspoon salt

MAKES 2 LOAVES

1 Sprinkle a baking sheet with flour. Mix the yeast with the water in a bowl. Place the French bread dough in a large bowl and break up. Add a little of the yeast water to soften the dough. Mix in a little of the bread flour, then alternate the additions of yeast water and both flours until incorporated. Sprinkle the salt over the dough and knead in. Turn out the dough onto a lightly floured surface and knead for about 5 minutes, until smooth and elastic.

2 Place in a lightly oiled bowl, cover with lightly oiled plastic wrap and let rise, in a warm place, for about 1 hour or until the dough has doubled in bulk.

3 Knock back the dough with your fist, then cover the bowl again with the oiled plastic wrap and let rise, in a warm place, for about 1 hour.

4 Divide the dough into 2 equal pieces, place on a lightly floured surface and stretch each piece into a baguette.

> **COOK'S TIP**
> You can use any amount up to 10 percent of previously made French baguette dough for this recipe. The épi can also be shaped into a circle to make an attractive crown.

5 Let the dough rest between rolling for a few minutes if necessary to avoid tearing. Pleat a floured dish towel on a baking sheet to make 2 molds for the loaves. Place them between the pleats of the towel, cover with lightly oiled plastic wrap and let rise, in a warm place, for 30 minutes.

6 Meanwhile, preheat the oven to 450°F. Using scissors, make diagonal cuts halfway through the dough about 2 inches apart, alternating the cuts along the loaf. Gently pull the dough in the opposite direction.

7 Place on the prepared baking sheet and bake for 20 minutes or until golden. Spray the inside of the oven with water 2–3 times during the first 5 minutes of baking. Transfer to a wire rack to cool.

4 cups white bread flour
2 teaspoons salt
1 tablespoon sugar
1/4 cup butter, softened
1/2 ounce fresh yeast
generous 1 cup lukewarm milk, plus
1 tablespoon extra milk, for glazing

MAKES 12 ROLLS

PETIT PAINS AU LAIT

These classic French round milk rolls have a soft crust and a light, slightly sweet crumb. They won't last long!

1 Lightly grease 2 baking sheets. Sift the flour and salt together into a large bowl. Stir in the sugar. Rub the softened butter into the flour.

2 Mix the yeast with 4 tablespoons of the milk. Stir in the remaining milk. Pour into the flour mixture and mix to a soft dough.

3 Turn out onto a lightly floured surface and knead for 8–10 minutes until smooth and elastic. Place in a lightly oiled bowl, cover with lightly oiled plastic wrap and let rise, in a warm place, for 1 hour or until doubled in bulk.

4 Turn out the dough onto a lightly floured surface and gently punch down. Divide into 12 equal pieces. Shape into balls and place on the baking sheets.

5 Using a sharp knife, cut a cross in the top of each roll. Cover with lightly oiled plastic wrap and let rise, in a warm place, for about 20 minutes or until doubled in size.

6 Preheat the oven to 400°F. Brush the rolls with milk and bake for 20–25 minutes or until golden. Transfer to a wire rack to cool.

---

3 1/2 cups white bread flour
1 1/2 teaspoons salt
1 teaspoon sugar
1/2 ounce fresh yeast
1/2 cup lukewarm milk
3/4 cup lukewarm water

MAKES 10 ROLLS

1 Lightly grease 2 baking sheets. Sift the flour and salt into a large bowl. Stir in the sugar and make a well in the center.

2 Mix the yeast with the milk until dissolved, then pour into the center of the flour mixture. Sprinkle on a little of the flour from around the edge. Let sit at room temperature for 15–20 minutes or until the mixture starts to bubble.

FRENCH DIMPLED ROLLS

A French and Belgian specialty, these attractive rolls are distinguished by the split down the center. They have a crusty finish while remaining soft and light inside—they taste great, too.

3 Add the water and gradually mix in the flour to form a fairly moist, soft dough. Turn out onto a lightly floured surface and knead for 8–10 minutes until smooth and elastic. Place in a lightly oiled bowl, cover with lightly oiled plastic wrap and let rise, at room temperature, for about 1 1/2 hours or until doubled in bulk.

4 Turn out onto a lightly floured surface and punch down. Re-cover and let rest for 5 minutes. Divide the dough into 10 pieces. Shape into balls by rolling the dough under a cupped hand, then roll until oval. Lightly flour the tops. Space apart on the baking sheets, cover with lightly oiled plastic wrap and let rise, at room temperature, for about 30 minutes or until almost doubled in size.

5 Lightly oil the side of your hand and press the center of each roll to make a deep split. Re-cover and let rest for 15 minutes. Meanwhile, place a roasting pan in the bottom of the oven and preheat the oven to 450°F. Pour 1 cup water into the pan and bake the rolls for 15 minutes or until golden. Transfer to a wire rack to cool.

KUGELHOPF

This inviting, fluted ring-shaped bread originates from Alsace, although Germany, Hungary and Austria all have their own variations of this popular recipe. Kugelhopf can be sweet or savory; this version is richly flavored with nuts, onion and bacon.

2/3 cup unsalted butter, softened
12 walnut halves
6 cups white bread flour
1 1/2 teaspoons salt
3/4 ounce fresh yeast
1 1/4 cups milk
4 ounces bacon, diced
1 onion, finely chopped
1 tablespoon vegetable oil
5 eggs, beaten
freshly ground black pepper

MAKES 1 LOAF

VARIATION

If you wish to make a sweet kugelhopf, replace the walnuts with whole almonds and the bacon and onion with 1 cup raisins and ⅓ cup mixed glacé fruits. Add ¼ cup sugar in step 2, and omit the black pepper.

1 Use 2 tablespoons of the butter to grease a 9-inch kugelhopf mold. Place 8 walnut halves around the base and chop the remainder.

2 Sift the flour and salt together into a large bowl and season with pepper. Make a well in the center. In a bowl, cream the yeast with 3 tablespoons of the milk. Pour into the center of the flour with the remaining milk. Mix in a little flour to make a thick batter. Sprinkle a little of the remaining flour on top of the batter, cover with plastic wrap and let sit in a warm place for 20–30 minutes, until the yeast mixture bubbles.

3 Meanwhile, fry the bacon and onion in the oil until the onion is pale golden.

4 Add the eggs to the flour mixture and gradually beat in the flour, using your hands. Gradually beat in the remaining softened butter to form a soft dough. Cover with lightly oiled plastic wrap and let rise, in a warm place, for 45–60 minutes or until almost doubled in bulk. Preheat the oven to 400°F.

5 Punch down the dough and gently knead in the bacon, onion and nuts. Place in the mold, cover with lightly oiled plastic wrap and let rise, in a warm place, for about 1 hour or until it has risen to the top of the mold.

6 Bake for 40–45 minutes or until the loaf has browned and sounds hollow when tapped on the bottom. Cool in the mold for 5 minutes, then on a wire rack.

BRIOCHE

Rich and buttery yet light and airy, this wonderful loaf captures the essence of the classic French bread.

1 Sift the flour and salt together into a large bowl and make a well in the center. Put the yeast in a measuring cup and stir in the milk.

2 Add the yeast mixture to the center of the flour with the eggs and combine to form a soft dough.

3 Using your hand, beat the dough for 4–5 minutes, until smooth and elastic. Cream the butter and sugar together. Gradually add the butter mixture to the dough in small amounts, making sure it is incorporated before adding more. Beat until smooth, shiny and elastic.

3 cups white bread flour
1/2 teaspoon salt
1/2 ounce fresh yeast
4 tablespoons lukewarm milk
3 eggs, lightly beaten
3/4 cup butter, softened
2 tablespoons sugar

FOR THE GLAZE
1 egg yolk
1 tablespoon milk

MAKES 1 LOAF

4 Cover the bowl with lightly oiled plastic wrap and let the dough rise, in a warm place, for 1–2 hours or until doubled in bulk.

5 Lightly punch down the dough, then re-cover and place in the refrigerator for 8–10 hours or overnight.

6 Lightly grease a scant 7-cup brioche mold. Turn the dough out onto a lightly floured surface. Cut off almost a quarter and set aside. Shape the rest into a ball and place in the prepared mold. Shape the reserved dough into an elongated egg shape. Using two or three fingers, make a hole in the center of the large ball of dough. Gently press the narrow end of the egg-shaped dough into the hole.

7 Combine the egg yolk and milk for the glaze, and brush a little on the brioche. Cover with lightly oiled plastic wrap and let rise, in a warm place, for 1½–2 hours or until the dough nearly reaches the top of the mold.

8 Meanwhile, preheat the oven to 450°F. Brush the brioche with the remaining glaze and bake for 10 minutes. Reduce the oven temperature to 375°F and bake for another 20–25 minutes or until golden. Turn out onto a wire rack to cool.

MEDITERRANEAN BREADS

The warm, rich flavors of the Mediterranean find their way into their breads. Olive oil, sun-dried tomatoes, olives, garlic and fresh herbs are all featured in breads that are so delicious they are now widely enjoyed all over the world. Ciabatta, panini all'olio rolls, focaccia and schiacciata are just a few examples. Spanish, Moroccan and Portuguese breads include local grains like corn and barley, together with seeds such as sesame, sunflower and pumpkin, giving breads an interesting taste and texture. Elaborate specialty breads are baked for religious festivals, the Christmas breads—christopsomo and Twelfth Night bread—being some of the most spectacular.

PUGLIESE

This classic Italian open-textured, soft-crumbed bread is moistened and flavored with fruity olive oil. Its floured top gives it a true country look.

FOR THE BIGA STARTER
1 1/2 cups white
bread flour
1/4 ounce fresh yeast
6 tablespoons lukewarm water

FOR THE DOUGH
2 cups white bread flour, plus extra
for dusting
2 cups whole-wheat bread flour
1 teaspoon sugar
2 teaspoons salt
1/2 ounce fresh yeast
generous 1 cup lukewarm water
5 tablespoons extra-virgin olive oil

MAKES 1 LARGE LOAF

VARIATION

Incorporate 1 cup chopped black olives into the dough at the end of step 5 for extra olive flavor.

1 Sift the flour for the *biga* starter into a large bowl. Make a well in the center. In a small bowl, cream the yeast with the water. Pour the liquid into the center of the flour and gradually mix in the surrounding flour to form a firm dough.

2 Turn the dough out onto a lightly floured surface and knead for 5 minutes until smooth and elastic. Return to the bowl, cover with lightly oiled plastic wrap and let rise, in a warm place, for 8–10 hours or until the dough has risen well and is starting to collapse.

3 Lightly flour a baking sheet. Mix the flours, sugar and salt for the dough in a large bowl. Cream the yeast and the water in another large bowl, then stir in the *biga* and combine.

4 Stir in the flour mixture a little at a time, then add the olive oil in the same way, and mix to a soft dough. Turn out onto a lightly floured surface and knead the dough for 8–10 minutes, until smooth and elastic.

5 Place in a lightly oiled bowl, cover with lightly oiled plastic wrap and let rise, in a warm place, for 1–1 1/2 hours or until doubled in bulk.

6 Turn out onto a lightly floured surface and punch down. Gently pull out the edges and fold under to make a round.

7 Transfer to the prepared baking sheet, cover with lightly oiled plastic wrap and let rise, in a warm place, for 1–1 1/2 hours or until almost doubled in size.

8 Meanwhile, preheat the oven to 450°F. Lightly dust the loaf with flour and bake for 15 minutes. Reduce the oven temperature to 400°F and bake for another 20 minutes or until the loaf sounds hollow when tapped on the bottom. Transfer to a wire rack to cool.

CIABATTA

This irregular-shaped Italian bread is so called because it looks like an old shoe or slipper. It is made with a very wet dough flavored with olive oil; baking produces a bread with holes and a wonderfully chewy crust.

1 Cream the yeast for the *biga* starter with a little of the water. Sift the flour into a large bowl. Gradually mix in the yeast mixture and enough of the remaining water to form a firm dough.

2 Turn out the *biga* starter dough onto a lightly floured surface and knead for about 5 minutes, until smooth and elastic. Return the dough to the bowl, cover with lightly oiled plastic wrap and let sit in a warm place for 12–15 hours or until the dough has risen and is starting to collapse.

3 Sprinkle 3 baking sheets with flour. Mix the yeast for the dough with a little of the water until creamy, then mix in the remainder. Add the yeast mixture to the *biga* and gradually mix in.

4 Mix in the milk, beating thoroughly with a wooden spoon. Using your hand, gradually beat in the flour, lifting the dough as you mix. Mixing the dough will take 15 minutes or more and form a very wet dough, impossible to knead on a work surface.

5 Beat in the salt and olive oil. Cover with lightly oiled plastic wrap and let rise, in a warm place, for 1½–2 hours or until doubled in bulk.

6 Using a spoon, carefully transfer one-third of the dough at a time to the prepared baking sheets, trying to avoid punching down the dough in the process.

7 Using floured hands, shape into rough oblong loaf shapes, about 1-inch thick. Flatten slightly with splayed fingers. Sprinkle with flour and let rise in a warm place for 30 minutes.

8 Meanwhile, preheat the oven to 425°F. Bake for 25–30 minutes or until golden brown and hollow-sounding when tapped on the bottom. Transfer to a wire rack to cool.

FOR THE BIGA STARTER
1/4 ounce fresh yeast
3/4–scant 1 cup lukewarm water
3 cups unbleached plain flour, plus extra for dusting

FOR THE DOUGH
1/2 ounce fresh yeast
1²/3 cups lukewarm water
4 tablespoons lukewarm milk
5 cups unbleached white bread flour
2 teaspoons salt
3 tablespoons extra virgin olive oil

MAKES 3 LOAVES

VARIATION
To make tomato-flavored ciabatta, add 1 cup oil-packed sun-dried tomatoes, drained and chopped. Add with the olive oil in step 5.

FOCACCIA

This simple dimple-topped Italian flat bread is punctuated with olive oil and the aromatic flavors of sage and garlic to produce a truly succulent loaf.

3/4 ounce fresh yeast
1 1/3–1 1/2 cups lukewarm water
3 tablespoons extra-virgin olive oil
5 cups white bread flour
2 teaspoons salt
1 tablespoon chopped fresh sage

FOR THE TOPPING
4 tablespoons extra-virgin olive oil
4 garlic cloves, chopped
12 fresh sage leaves

MAKES 2 ROUND LOAVES

VARIATION

Flavor the bread with other fresh herbs, such as oregano, basil or rosemary, and top with chopped black olives.

4 Punch down the dough and turn out onto a lightly floured surface. Gently knead in the chopped sage. Divide the dough into 2 equal pieces. Shape each into a ball, roll out into 10-inch circles and place in the prepared pans.

1 Lightly oil 2 10-inch shallow round cake pans or pizza pans. Mix the yeast with 4 tablespoons of the water, then stir in the remaining water. Stir in the oil.

2 Sift the flour and salt together into a large bowl and make a well in the center. Pour the yeast mixture into the well in the center of the flour and mix to a soft dough.

3 Turn out the dough onto a lightly floured surface and knead for 8–10 minutes, until smooth and elastic. Place in a lightly oiled bowl, cover with lightly oiled plastic wrap or a large, lightly oiled plastic bag, and let rise, in a warm place, for 1–1 1/2 hours or until the dough has doubled in bulk.

5 Cover with lightly oiled plastic wrap and let rise in a warm place for about 30 minutes. Uncover and, using your fingertips, poke the dough to make deep dimples over the entire surface. Replace the plastic wrap cover and let rise until doubled in bulk.

6 Meanwhile, preheat the oven to 400°F. Drizzle on the olive oil for the topping and sprinkle each focaccia evenly with chopped garlic. Dot the sage leaves on the surface. Bake for 25–30 minutes or until both loaves are golden. Immediately remove the focaccia from the pans and transfer them to a wire rack to cool slightly. These loaves are best served warm.

2 cups white bread flour
1½ teaspoons salt
½ ounce fresh yeast
scant ⅔ cup lukewarm water
2 tablespoons extra-virgin olive oil,
plus extra for brushing
sesame seeds, for coating

MAKES 20 GRISSINI

1½ cups unbleached white flour
1 teaspoon salt
1 tablespoon olive oil
7 tablespoons lukewarm water

MAKES 4 PIADINE

SESAME-STUDDED GRISSINI

These crisp, pencil-like breadsticks are easy to make and far more delicious than the commercially manufactured grissini. Once you start to nibble one, it will be difficult to stop.

1 Lightly oil 2 baking sheets. Sift the flour and salt together into a large bowl and make a well in the center.

2 In a bowl, cream the yeast with the water. Pour into the center of the flour, add the olive oil and mix to a soft dough. Turn out onto a lightly floured surface and knead for 8–10 minutes, until smooth and elastic.

3 Roll the dough into a rectangle about 6 × 8 inches. Brush with olive oil, cover with lightly oiled plastic wrap and let rise, in a warm place, for about 1 hour or until doubled in bulk.

4 Preheat the oven to 400°F. Spread out the sesame seeds. Cut the dough in two 3 x 4-inch rectangles. Cut each piece into ten 3-inch strips. Stretch each strip gently until it is about 12 inches long.

5 Roll each grissini, as it is made, in the sesame seeds. Place the grissini on the prepared baking sheets, spaced well apart. Lightly brush with olive oil. let rise, in a warm place, for 10 minutes, then bake for 15–20 minutes. Transfer to a wire rack to cool.

PIADINE

These soft unleavened Italian breads, cooked directly on a griddle, were originally cooked on a hot stone over an open fire. They are best eaten while still warm. Try them as an accompaniment to soups and dips.

1 Sift the flour and salt together into a large bowl; make a well in the center.

2 Add the olive oil and water to the center of the flour and gradually mix in to form a dough. Knead on a lightly floured surface for 4–5 minutes, until smooth and elastic. Place in a lightly oiled bowl, cover with oiled plastic wrap and let rest for 20 minutes.

3 Heat a griddle over a medium heat. Divide the dough into 4 equal pieces and roll each into an 7-inch round. Cover until ready to cook.

4 Lightly oil the hot griddle, add 1 or 2 piadine and cook for about 2 minutes or until they are starting to brown. Turn the piadine over and cook for another 1–1½ minutes. Serve warm.

PANETTONE

This classic Italian bread can be found throughout Italy around Christmas. It is a surprisingly light bread, even though it is rich with butter and dried fruit.

3½ cups white bread flour
½ teaspoon salt
½ ounce fresh yeast
½ cup lukewarm milk
2 eggs
2 eggs yolks
6 tablespoons sugar
⅔ cup butter, softened
⅔ cup mixed chopped peel
½ cup raisins
melted butter, for brushing

MAKES 1 LOAF

COOK'S TIP
Once the dough has been enriched with butter, do not prove in too warm a place or the loaf will become greasy.

1 Using a double layer of waxed paper, line and butter a 6-inch deep cake pan or soufflé dish. Leave 3 inches of paper above the top of the pan.

2 Sift the flour and salt together into a large bowl. Make a well in the center. Mix the yeast with 4 tablespoons of the milk, then mix in the remainder.

3 Pour the yeast mixture into the center of the flour, add the whole eggs and mix in sufficient flour to make a thick batter. Sprinkle a little of the remaining flour over the top and let "sponge," in a warm place, for 30 minutes.

4 Add the egg yolks and sugar and mix to a soft dough. Work in the softened butter, then turn out on to a lightly floured surface and knead for 5 minutes until smooth and elastic. Place in a lightly oiled bowl, cover with lightly oiled plastic wrap and let rise, in a slightly warm place, for 1½–2 hours, or until doubled in bulk.

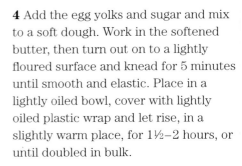

5 Punch down the dough and turn out onto a lightly floured surface. Gently knead in the peel and raisins. Shape into a ball and place in the prepared pan. Cover with lightly oiled plastic wrap and let rise, in a slightly warm place, for about 1 hour or until doubled.

6 Meanwhile, preheat the oven to 375°F. Brush the surface with melted butter and cut a cross in the top using a sharp knife. Bake for 20 minutes, then reduce the oven temperature to 350°F. Brush the top with butter again and bake for another 25–30 minutes or until golden. Cool in the pan for 5–10 minutes, then turn out onto a wire rack to cool.

PANE AL CIOCCOLATO

This slightly sweet chocolate bread from Italy is often served with creamy mascarpone cheese as a dessert or snack. The dark chocolate pieces add texture to this light loaf.

3 cups white bread flour
1 ½ tablespoons cocoa powder
½ teaspoon salt
2 tablespoons sugar
½ ounce fresh yeast
1 cup lukewarm water
2 tablespoons butter, softened
3 ounces semi-sweet chocolate, coarsely chopped
melted butter, for brushing

MAKES 1 LOAF

1 Lightly grease a 6-inch round deep cake pan. Sift the flour, cocoa powder and salt together into a large bowl. Stir in the sugar. Make a well in the center.

2 In a small bowl, mix the yeast with 4 tablespoons of the water, then stir in the rest. Add to the center of the flour mixture and gradually mix to a dough.

3 Knead in the softened butter, then knead on a floured surface until smooth and elastic. Place in a lightly oiled bowl, cover with lightly oiled plastic wrap and let rise, in a warm place, for about 1 hour or until doubled in bulk.

6 Preheat the oven to 425°F. Bake for 10 minutes, then reduce the oven temperature to 375°F and bake for another 25–30 minutes. Brush the top with melted butter and let cool on a wire rack.

VARIATION
You can also shape this bread into one large or two small rounds and bake on a lightly greased baking sheet. Reduce the baking time by about 10 minutes.

4 Turn out onto a lightly floured surface and punch down. Gently knead in the chocolate, then cover with lightly oiled plastic wrap; let rest for 5 minutes.

5 Shape the dough into a round and place in the pan. Cover with lightly oiled plastic wrap and let rise, in a warm place, for 45 minutes or until doubled; the dough should reach the top of the pan.

SCHIACCIATA

This Tuscan version of Italian pizza-style flat bread can be rolled to varying thicknesses to give either a crisp or soft, bread-like finish.

3 cups white bread flour
½ teaspoon salt
½ ounce fresh yeast
scant 1 cup lukewarm water
4 tablespoons extra-virgin olive oil

FOR THE TOPPING
2 tablespoons extra-virgin olive oil,
for brushing
2 tablespoons fresh rosemary leaves
coarse sea salt, for sprinkling

MAKES 1 LARGE LOAF

1 Lightly oil a baking sheet. Sift the flour and salt into a large bowl and make a well in the center. Mix the yeast with half the water. Add to the center of the flour with the remaining water and olive oil and mix to a soft dough. Turn out the dough onto a lightly floured surface and knead for 10 minutes, until smooth and elastic.

2 Place in a lightly oiled bowl, cover with lightly oiled plastic wrap and let rise, in a warm place, for about 1 hour or until doubled in bulk.

3 Punch down the dough, turn out onto a lightly floured surface and knead gently. Roll out to a 12 × 8-inch rectangle and place on the prepared baking sheet. Brush with some of the olive oil for the topping and cover with lightly oiled plastic wrap.

4 Let rise, in a warm place, for about 20 minutes, then brush with the remaining oil, prick all over with a fork and sprinkle with rosemary and sea salt. Let rise again in a warm place for 15 minutes.

5 Meanwhile, preheat the oven to 400°F. Bake for 30 minutes or until light golden. Transfer to a wire rack to cool slightly. Serve warm.

PORTUGUESE CORN BREAD

While the Spanish make a corn bread with barley flour, the Portuguese use white flour and cornmeal. This tempting version has a hard crust with a moist, mouthwatering crumb. It slices beautifully and tastes wonderful served simply with butter or olive oil, or with cheese.

¾ ounce fresh yeast
1 cup lukewarm water
2 cups yellow cornmeal
4 cups white bread flour
⅔ cup lukewarm milk
2 tablespoons olive oil
1½ teaspoons salt
polenta, for dusting

MAKES 1 LARGE LOAF

1 Dust a baking sheet with a little cornmeal. Put the yeast in a large bowl and gradually mix in the lukewarm water until smooth. Stir in half the cornmeal and ½ cup of the flour and mix to a batter, with a wooden spoon.

6 Turn out the dough onto a lightly floured surface and punch down. Shape into a round ball, flatten slightly and place on the prepared baking sheet. Dust with polenta, cover with a large upturned bowl and let rise, in a warm place, for about 1 hour or until doubled in size. Meanwhile, preheat the oven to 450°F.

VARIATION
Replace 50 percent of the yellow cornmeal with polenta for a rougher textured, slightly crunchier loaf.

7 Bake for 10 minutes, spraying the inside of the oven with water 2–3 times. Reduce the oven temperature to 375°F and bake for another 20–25 minutes or until golden and hollow sounding when tapped on the bottom. Transfer to a wire rack to cool.

2 Cover the bowl with lightly oiled plastic wrap and let the batter sit undisturbed in a warm place for about 30 minutes or until bubbles start to appear on the surface. Remove the plastic wrap.

3 Stir the milk into the batter, then stir in the olive oil. Gradually mix in the remaining cornmeal, flour and salt to form a pliable dough.

4 Turn out the dough onto a lightly floured surface and knead for about 10 minutes, until smooth and elastic.

5 Place in a lightly oiled bowl, cover with lightly oiled plastic wrap and let rise, in a warm place, for 1½–2 hours or until doubled in bulk.

PAN GALLEGO

3 cups white bread flour
1 cup whole-wheat bread flour
2 teaspoons salt
¾ ounce fresh yeast
generous 1 cup lukewarm water
2 tablespoons olive oil or melted lard
2 tablespoons pumpkin seeds
2 tablespoons sunflower seeds
1 tablespoon millet
yellow cornmeal, for dusting

MAKES 1 LARGE LOAF

Here, a typical round bread with a twisted top from Galicia. The olive oil gives a soft crumb, and the millet, pumpkin and sunflower seeds scattered through the loaf provide an interesting mix of textures.

COOK'S TIP
You can replace the fresh yeast with a ¼ ounce envelope of easy-blend dried yeast. Stir into the flours in step 1. Continue as in the recipe.

1 Sprinkle a baking sheet with cornmeal. Combine the flours and salt in a large bowl.

2 In a small bowl, mix the yeast with the water. Add to the center of the flours with the olive oil or melted lard and mix into a firm dough. Turn out onto a lightly floured surface and knead for about 10 minutes, until smooth and elastic. Place in a lightly oiled bowl, then cover with lightly oiled plastic wrap and let rise, in a warm place, for 1½–2 hours or until doubled in bulk.

3 Punch down the dough and turn out onto a lightly floured surface. Gently knead in the pumpkin seeds, sunflower seeds and millet. Re-cover and let rest for 5 minutes.

4 Shape into a round ball; twist the center to make a cap. Transfer to the prepared baking sheet and dust with cornmeal. Cover with a large upturned bowl and let rise, in a warm place, for 45 minutes or until doubled in bulk.

5 Meanwhile, place an empty roasting pan in the bottom of the oven. Preheat the oven to 425°F. Pour about 1¼ cups cold water into the roasting pan. Lift the bowl off the risen loaf and immediately place the baking sheet in the oven, above the roasting pan. Bake the bread for 10 minutes.

6 Remove the pan of water and bake the bread for another 25–30 minutes or until well browned and hollow-sounding when tapped on the bottom. Transfer to a wire rack to cool.

PAN DE CEBADA

This Spanish country bread has a close, heavy texture and is quite satisfying.
It is richly flavored, incorporating barley flour and yellow cornmeal.

FOR THE SOURDOUGH STARTER
1½ cups cornmeal
scant 2½ cups water
2 cups whole-wheat flour
¾ cup barley flour

FOR THE DOUGH
¾ ounce fresh yeast
3 tablespoons lukewarm water
2 cups whole-wheat flour
1 tablespoon salt
cornmeal, for dusting

MAKES 1 LARGE LOAF

1 In a saucepan, mix the cornmeal for the sourdough starter with half the water, then blend in the remainder. Cook over low heat, stirring continuously, until thickened. Transfer to a large bowl and set aside to cool.

2 Mix in the whole-wheat flour and barley flour. Turn out onto a lightly floured surface and knead for 5 minutes. Return to the bowl, cover with lightly oiled plastic wrap and let the starter sit in a warm place for 36 hours.

5 Punch down the dough and turn out onto a lightly floured surface. Shape into a plump round. Sprinkle with a little cornmeal.

6 Place the shaped bread on the prepared baking sheet. Cover with a large upturned bowl. Let rise, in a warm place, for about 1 hour or until nearly doubled in bulk. Place an empty roasting pan in the bottom of the oven. Preheat the oven to 425°F.

7 Pour 1¼ cups cold water into the roasting pan. Lift the bowl off the risen loaf and immediately place the baking sheet in the oven. Bake the bread for 10 minutes. Remove the pan of water, reduce the oven temperature to 375°F and bake for about 20 minutes. Cool on a wire rack.

3 Dust a baking sheet with cornmeal. In a small bowl, mix the yeast with the water for the dough. Mix the yeast mixture into the starter with the whole-wheat flour and salt and work into a dough. Turn out on to a lightly floured surface and knead for 4–5 minutes, until smooth and elastic.

4 Transfer the dough to a lightly oiled bowl, cover with lightly oiled plastic wrap or an oiled plastic bag and let sit, in a warm place, for 1½–2 hours or until nearly doubled in bulk.

TWELFTH NIGHT BREAD

4 cups white bread flour
½ teaspoon salt
1 ounce yeast
scant ⅔ cup mixed lukewarm milk
and water
6 tablespoons butter
6 tablespoons sugar
2 teaspoons finely grated
lemon zest
2 teaspoons finely grated
orange zest
2 eggs
1 tablespoon brandy
1 tablespoon orange flower water
silver coin or dried bean
(optional)
1 egg white, lightly beaten,
for glazing

FOR THE DECORATION
a mixture of candied fruit slices
flaked almonds

MAKES 1 LARGE LOAF

COOK'S TIP
If desired, this bread can be baked
in a lightly greased 9½-inch
ring-shaped cake pan or savarin
mold. Place the dough seam-side
down into the pan or mold and seal
the ends together.

January 6th, Epiphany or the Day of the Three Kings, is celebrated in Spain as a time to exchange Christmas presents. Historically this date was when the Three Wise Men arrived bearing gifts. An ornamental bread ring is specially baked for the occasion. The traditional version contains a silver coin, china figure or dried bean hidden inside—the lucky recipient is declared King of the festival!

2 In a bowl, mix the yeast with the milk and water until the yeast has dissolved. Pour the yeast mixture into the center of the flour and stir in enough of the flour from around the sides of the bowl to make a thick batter.

3 Sprinkle a little of the remaining flour over the top of the batter and let "sponge," in a warm place, for about 15 minutes or until frothy.

4 Using an electric whisk or a wooden spoon, beat the butter and sugar together in a bowl until soft and creamy, then set aside.

5 Add the citrus zest, eggs, brandy and orange flower water to the flour mixture and use a wooden spoon to mix into a sticky dough.

6 Using one hand, beat the mixture until it forms a fairly smooth dough. Gradually beat in the reserved butter mixture and beat for a few minutes, until the dough is smooth and elastic. Cover with lightly oiled plastic wrap and let rise, in a warm place, for about 1½ hours or until doubled in bulk.

7 Punch down the dough and turn out onto a lightly floured surface. Gently knead for 2 or 3 minutes, incorporating the lucky coin or bean, if using.

8 Using a rolling pin, roll out the dough into a long strip measuring about 26 × 5 inches.

9 Roll up the dough from one long side like a Swiss roll to make a long sausage shape. Place seam side down on the prepared baking sheet and seal the ends together. Cover with lightly oiled plastic wrap and let rise, in a warm place, for 1–1½ hours or until doubled in size.

10 Meanwhile, preheat the oven to 350°F. Brush the dough ring with lightly beaten egg white and decorate with candied fruit slices, pushing them slightly into the dough. Sprinkle with almonds and bake for 30–35 minutes or until risen and golden. Turn out onto a wire rack to cool.

1 Lightly grease a large baking sheet. Sift the flour and salt together into a large bowl. Make a well in the center.

MALLORCAN ENSAIMADAS

2 cups white bread flour
½ teaspoon salt
¼ cup sugar
½ ounce fresh yeast
5 tablespoons lukewarm milk
1 egg
2 tablespoons sunflower oil
¼ cup butter, melted
confectioners' sugar, for dusting

MAKES 16 ROLLS

These spiral-or snail-shaped rolls are a popular Spanish breakfast treat. Traditionally, lard or saim *was used to brush over the strips of sweetened dough, but nowadays mainly butter is used to add a delicious richness.*

1 Lightly grease 2 baking sheets. Sift the flour and salt together into a large mixing bowl. Stir in the sugar and make a well in the center.

2 In a small bowl, mix the yeast with the milk, pour into the center of the flour mixture, then sprinkle a little of the flour mixture evenly on top of the liquid. Let sit in a warm place for about 15 minutes or until frothy.

3 In a small bowl, beat the egg and sunflower oil together. Add to the flour mixture and mix to a smooth dough.

4 Turn out onto a lightly floured surface and knead for 8–10 minutes. until smooth and elastic. Place in a lightly oiled bowl, cover with lightly oiled plastic wrap and let rise, in a warm place, for 1 hour or until doubled in bulk.

5 Turn out the dough onto a lightly floured surface. Punch down and divide the dough into 16 equal pieces. Shape each piece into a thin rope about 15 inches long. Pour the melted butter onto a plate and dip the ropes into the butter to coat.

6 On the baking sheets, curl each rope into a loose spiral, spacing well apart. Tuck the ends under to seal. Cover with lightly oiled plastic wrap and let rise, in a warm place, for about 45 minutes or until doubled in size.

7 Meanwhile, preheat the oven to 375°F. Brush the rolls with water and dust with confectioners' sugar. Bake for 10 minutes or until light golden brown. Cool on a wire rack. Dust again with confectioners' sugar and serve warm.

PITA BREAD

*These Turkish breads are a favorite in both the eastern Mediterranean
and the Middle East, and have are popular in England and the United States.
This versatile soft, flat bread forms a pocket as it cooks,
making it perfect for filling with vegetables, salads or meats.*

*2 cups white bread flour
1 teaspoon salt
1/2 ounce fresh yeast
scant 2/3 cup lukewarm water
2 teaspoons extra-virgin olive oil*

MAKES 6 PITA BREADS

VARIATIONS
To make whole-wheat pita breads,
replace half the white flour
with whole-wheat flour. You
can also make smaller round pita
breads about 4 inches in diameter
to serve as snack breads.

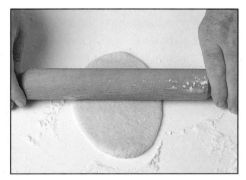

5 Roll out each ball of dough in turn to
an oval about 1/4-inch thick and 6 inches
long. Place on a floured dish towel
and cover with lightly oiled plastic wrap.
Let rise at room temperature for
20–30 minutes.

6 Meanwhile, preheat the oven to 450°F.
Place 3 baking sheets in the oven to
heat at the same time.

1 Sift the flour and salt together into a
bowl. In a small bowl, mix the yeast with
the water until dissolved, then stir in the
olive oil and pour into a large bowl.

2 Gradually beat the flour into the yeast
mixture, then knead the mixture to
make a soft dough.

3 Turn out onto a lightly floured surface
and knead for 5 minutes until smooth
and elastic. Place in a large clean bowl,
cover with lightly oiled plastic wrap
and let rise, in a warm place, for about
1 hour or until doubled in bulk.

4 Punch down the dough. On a lightly
floured surface, divide it into 6 equal
pieces and shape into balls. Cover with
oiled plastic wrap; let rest for 5 minutes.

7 Place two pita breads on each baking
sheet and bake for 4–6 minutes or until
puffed up; they do not need to brown. If
preferred, cook the pita bread in batches.
It is important that the oven has reached
the recommended temperature before
the pita breads are baked. This ensures
that they will puff up.

8 Transfer the pitas to a wire rack to
cool until warm, then cover with a dish
towel to keep them soft.

NORTH EUROPEAN AND SCANDINAVIAN BREADS

The northern Europeans and Scandinavians make many different breads, from German sourdough bread with its distinctive flavor to the light-crumbed Swiss braid. Also, from these northern climes, come the famous Swedish crispbreads, Russian potato bread and blinis, lightly scented saffron buns and port-flavored rye bread. Christmas breads are enriched with fruit, while Bulgaria has its own poppy-seeded circular bread for religious festivals.

SWISS BRAID

This braided, attractively tapered loaf is known as zupfe *in Switzerland. Often eaten on weekends, it has a glossy crust and a wonderfully light crumb.*

3 cups white flour
1 teaspoon salt
¾ ounce fresh yeast
2 tablespoons lukewarm water
⅔ cup sour cream
1 egg, lightly beaten
¼ cup butter, softened

For the Glaze
1 egg yolk
1 tablespoon water

Makes 1 Loaf

COOK'S TIP
If you prefer, use a ¼ ounce envelope of easy-blend dried yeast. Add directly to the flour with the salt, then add the warmed sour cream and water and combine.

1 Lightly grease a baking sheet. Sift the flour and salt together into a large bowl and make a well in the center. Mix the yeast with the water in a small bowl.

2 Gently warm the sour cream in a small pan until it reaches 98.6°F. Add to the yeast mixture and combine.

3 Add the yeast mixture and egg to the center of the flour and gradually mix into a dough. Beat in the softened butter.

4 Turn out onto a lightly floured surface and knead for 5 minutes, until smooth and elastic. Place in a lightly oiled bowl, cover with lightly oiled plastic wrap and let rise, in a warm place, for about 1½ hours or until doubled in size.

5 Turn out onto a lightly floured surface and punch down. Cut in half and shape each piece of dough into a long rope about 14 inches in length.

6 To make the braid, place the two pieces of dough on top of each other to form a cross. Starting with the bottom rope, fold the top end over and place between the two bottom ropes. Fold the remaining top rope over so that all four ropes are pointing downward. Starting from the left, braid the first rope over the second, and the third rope over the fourth.

7 Continue braiding in this way to form a tapered bread. Tuck the ends underneath and place on the prepared baking sheet. Cover with lightly oiled plastic wrap and let rise, in a warm place, for about 40 minutes.

8 Meanwhile, preheat the oven to 375°F. Mix the egg yolk and water for the glaze, and brush over the loaf. Bake the bread for 30–35 minutes or until golden. Cool on a wire rack.

GERMAN SOURDOUGH BREAD

This bread includes rye, whole-wheat and all-purpose flours for a superb depth of flavor. Serve it cut in thick slices, with creamy butter or a sharp cheese.

FOR THE SOURDOUGH STARTER
3/4 cup rye flour
1/3 cup warm water
pinch caraway seeds

FOR THE DOUGH
1/2 ounce fresh yeast
1 1/3 cups lukewarm water
2 1/2 cups rye flour
1 1/4 cups whole-wheat flour
1 1/4 cups all-purpose flour
2 teaspoons salt

MAKES 1 LOAF

1 Combine the rye flour, warm water and caraway for the starter in a large bowl with your fingertips, to make a soft paste. Cover with a damp dish towel and let sit in a warm place for about 36 hours. Stir after 24 hours.

2 Lightly grease a baking sheet. In a measuring cup, blend the yeast for the dough with the lukewarm water. Add to the starter and mix thoroughly.

5 Turn out onto a lightly floured surface, punch down and knead gently. Shape into a round and place in a floured basket, or *couronne*, with the seam up. Cover with lightly oiled plastic wrap and let rise, in a warm place, for 2–3 hours.

6 Meanwhile, preheat the oven to 400°F. Turn out the loaf onto the prepared baking sheet and bake for 35–40 minutes. Cool on a wire rack.

COOK'S TIP
Proofing the dough in a floured basket or *couronne* gives it its characteristic patterned crust, but is not essential. Make sure that you flour the basket well, otherwise the dough may stick.

3 Mix the rye flour, whole-wheat bread flour and all-purpose flour for the dough with the salt in a large bowl; make a well in the center. Pour in the yeast liquid and gradually incorporate the surrounding flour to make a smooth dough.

4 Turn out the dough on to a lightly floured surface and knead for 8–10 minutes until smooth and elastic. Place in a lightly oiled bowl, cover with lightly oiled plastic wrap and let rise, in a warm place, for 1 1/2 hours, or until nearly doubled in bulk.

STOLLEN

This German specialty bread, made for the Christmas season, is rich with rum-soaked fruits and is wrapped around a moist almond filling. The folded shape of the dough over the filling represents the baby Jesus wrapped in swaddling clothes.

1/2 cup golden raisins
1/4 cup currants
3 tablespoons rum
3 1/4 cups white flour
1/2 teaspoon salt
1/4 cup sugar
1/4 teaspoon ground cardamom
1/2 teaspoon ground cinnamon
1 1/2 ounces fresh yeast
1/2 cup lukewarm milk
1/4 cup butter, melted
1 egg, lightly beaten
1/3 cup mixed chopped peel
1/3 cup blanched whole almonds, chopped
melted butter, for brushing
confectioners' sugar, for dusting

FOR THE ALMOND FILLING
1 cup ground almonds
1/4 cup sugar
1/2 cup confectioners' sugar
1/2 teaspoon fresh lemon juice
1/2 egg, lightly beaten

MAKES 1 LARGE LOAF

COOK'S TIP
You can dust the cooled stollen with confectioners' sugar and cinnamon, or drizzle over a thin glacé icing.

1 Lightly grease a baking sheet. Preheat the oven to 350°F. Put the golden raisins and currants in a heatproof bowl and warm for 3–4 minutes. Pour in the rum and set aside.

2 Sift the flour and salt together into a large bowl. Stir in the sugar and spices.

3 In a small bowl, mix the yeast with the milk until creamy. Pour into the flour and mix a little of the flour from around the edge into the milk mixture to make a thick batter. Sprinkle some of the remaining flour on top of the batter, then cover with plastic wrap and let sit in a warm place for 30 minutes.

4 Add the melted butter and egg and mix into a soft dough. Turn out the dough onto a lightly floured surface and knead for 8–10 minutes, until smooth and elastic. Place in a lightly oiled bowl, cover with lightly oiled plastic wrap and let rise, in a warm place, for 2–3 hours or until doubled in bulk.

5 Combine the ground almonds and sugars for the filling. Add the lemon juice and enough egg to knead to a smooth paste. Shape into an 8-inch long sausage, cover and set aside.

6 Turn out the dough onto a lightly floured surface and punch down.

7 Pat out the dough into a rectangle about 1 inch thick and sprinkle on the golden raisins, currants, mixed chopped peel and almonds. Fold and knead the dough to incorporate the fruit and nuts.

8 Roll out the dough into an oval about 12 × 9 inches. Roll the center slightly thinner than the edges. Place the almond paste filling along the center and fold over the dough to enclose it, making sure that the top of the dough doesn't completely cover the base. The top edge should be slightly in from the bottom edge. Press down to seal.

9 Place the loaf on the prepared baking sheet, cover with lightly oiled plastic wrap and let rise, in a warm place, for 45–60 minutes or until doubled in size.

10 Meanwhile, preheat the oven to 400°F. Bake the loaf for about 30 minutes or until it sounds hollow when tapped on the bottom. Brush the top with melted butter and transfer to a wire rack to cool. Dust with confectioners' sugar just before serving.

BUCHTY

Popular in both Poland and Germany as breakfast treats, these are also excellent split and toasted, and served with cured meats.

4 cups white flour
1 teaspoon salt
¼ cup sugar
scant ½ cup butter
½ cup milk
¾ ounce fresh yeast
3 eggs, lightly beaten
3 tablespoons butter, melted
confectioners' sugar, for dusting
(optional)

MAKES 16 ROLLS

COOK'S TIP

If you do not have a square pan use a round one. Place 2 rolls in the center and the rest around the edge.

1 Grease an 8-inch square pan, (preferably with a removable bottom). Sift the flour and salt together into a large bowl and stir in the sugar. Make a well in the center.

2 Melt ¼ cup of the butter in a small pan, then remove from the heat and stir in the milk. Let cool until lukewarm. Stir the yeast into the milk mixture until it has dissolved.

3 Pour into the center of the flour and stir in enough flour to form a thick batter. Sprinkle with a little of the surrounding flour, cover and let sit in a warm place for 30 minutes.

4 Gradually beat in the eggs and remaining flour to form a soft, smooth dough. This will take about 10 minutes. Cover with lightly oiled plastic wrap and let rise, in a warm place, for about 1½ hours or until doubled in bulk.

5 Turn out the dough onto a lightly floured surface and punch down. Divide into 16 equal pieces and shape into rounds. Melt the remaining butter, roll the rounds in it to coat, then place, slightly apart, in the pan. Cover with lightly oiled plastic wrap and let rise, in a warm place, for about 1 hour or until doubled.

6 Meanwhile, preheat the oven to 375°F. Spoon any remaining melted butter evenly over the rolls and bake for 25 minutes or until golden brown. Turn out onto a wire rack to cool. If serving buchty as a breakfast bread, dust the loaf with confectioners' sugar before separating it into rolls.

POLISH RYE BREAD

*This rye bread is made with half white flour, which gives it a lighter, more
open texture than a traditional rye loaf. Served thinly sliced, it is the perfect
accompaniment for cold meats and fish.*

2 cups rye flour
2 cups white flour
2 teaspoons caraway seeds
2 teaspoons salt
¾ ounce fresh yeast
scant ⅔ cup lukewarm milk
1 teaspoon honey
scant ⅔ cup lukewarm water
whole-wheat flour, for dusting

MAKES 1 LOAF

1 Lightly grease a baking sheet. Mix the flours, caraway seeds and salt in a large bowl and make a well in the center.

2 In a small bowl or measuring cup, mix the yeast with the milk and honey. Pour into the center of the flour, add the water and gradually incorporate the surrounding flour and caraway mixture until a dough forms.

3 Turn out the dough onto a lightly floured surface and knead for 8–10 minutes, until smooth, elastic and firm. Place in a large, lightly oiled bowl, cover with lightly oiled plastic wrap and let rise, in a warm place, for about 3 hours or until doubled in bulk.

4 Turn out the dough onto a lightly floured surface and punch down. Shape into an oval loaf and place on the prepared baking sheet.

5 Dust with whole-wheat flour, cover with lightly oiled plastic wrap and let rise, in a warm place, for 1–1½ hours or until doubled in size. Meanwhile, preheat the oven to 425°F.

6 Using a sharp knife, slash the loaf with two long cuts about 1 inch apart. Bake for 30–35 minutes or until the loaf sounds hollow when tapped on the bottom. Transfer the loaf to a wire rack and set aside to cool.

6 cups white flour
2 teaspoons salt
1 ounce fresh yeast
½ cup lukewarm milk
1 teaspoon honey
2 eggs
⅔ cup plain yogurt
¼ cup butter, melted
beaten egg, for glazing
poppy seeds, for sprinkling

MAKES 1 LARGE LOAF

VARIATION
For a special finish, divide the dough into 3 equal pieces, roll into long thin strips and braid together, starting with the center of the strips. Once braided, shape into a circle and seal the ends together. Make sure that the hole in the center is quite large, otherwise the hole will fill in as the bread rises.

KOLACH

Often prepared for religious celebrations and family feasts, this Bulgarian bread gets its name from its circular shape—kolo, which means circle. It has a golden crust sprinkled with poppy seeds and a moist crumb, which makes this loaf a very good keeper.

1 Grease a large baking sheet. Sift the flour and salt together into a large bowl and make a well in the center.

2 In a small bowl, mix the yeast with the milk and honey. Add to the center of the flour with the eggs, yogurt and melted butter. Gradually mix into the flour to form a firm dough.

3 Turn out onto a lightly floured surface and knead for 8–10 minutes, until smooth and elastic. Place in a lightly oiled bowl, cover with lightly oiled plastic wrap or slip into an oiled plastic bag. let rise, in a warm place, for 1½ hours or until doubled in bulk.

4 Punch down the dough and turn out onto a lightly floured surface. Knead lightly and shape into a ball. Place seam side down and make a hole in the center with your fingers.

5 Gradually enlarge the cavity, turning the dough to make a 10-inch circle. Transfer to the baking sheet, cover with lightly oiled plastic wrap and let rise, in a warm place, for 30–45 minutes or until doubled in size.

6 Meanwhile, preheat the oven to 400°F. Brush the loaf with beaten egg and sprinkle with poppy seeds. Bake for 35 minutes or until golden. Cool on a wire rack.

BLINIS

Blinis are the celebrated leavened Russian pancakes. Traditionally served with sour cream and caviar, they have a very distinctive flavor and a fluffy, light texture.

½ cup buckwheat flour
½ cup all-purpose flour
½ teaspoon freshly ground black pepper
1 teaspoon salt
½ ounce fresh yeast
scant 1 cup lukewarm milk
1 egg, separated

MAKES ABOUT 10 BLINIS

VARIATION
You can use all buckwheat flour, which will give the blinis a stronger flavor.

1 Combine the buckwheat flour, plain flour, pepper and salt in a large bowl.

2 In a small bowl, mix the yeast with 4 tablespoons of the milk, then mix in the remaining milk.

3 Add the egg yolk to the flour mixture and gradually whisk in the yeast mixture to form a smooth batter. Cover with plastic wrap and let stand in a warm place for 1 hour.

4 Whisk the egg white until it forms soft peaks and fold into the batter. Lightly oil a heavy frying pan and heat it.

5 Add about 3 tablespoons of the batter to make a 4-inch round pancake. Cook until the surface begins to dry out, then turn the pancake over using a spatula and cook for 1–2 minutes. Repeat with the remaining batter. Serve warm.

POPPY SEED ROLL

A favorite sweet yeast bread in both Poland and Hungary, this has an unusual filling of poppy seeds, almonds, raisins and glacé fruit spiraling through the dough.

3 cups white flour
½ teaspoon salt
2 tablespoons sugar
¾ ounce fresh yeast
½ cup lukewarm milk
1 egg, lightly beaten
¼ cup butter, melted
1 tablespoon toasted sliced almonds

FOR THE FILLING
⅔ cup poppy seeds
¼ cup butter
6 tablespoons sugar
½ cup raisins
½ cup ground almonds
⅓ cup mixed chopped glacé fruit,
finely chopped
½ teaspoon ground cinnamon

FOR THE ICING
1 cup confectioners' sugar
1 tablespoon fresh lemon juice
2–3 teaspoons water

MAKES 1 LARGE LOAF

1 Lightly grease a baking sheet. Sift the flour and salt together into a large bowl. Stir in the sugar. Mix the yeast with the milk. Add to the flour with the egg and melted butter and mix into a dough.

2 Turn out onto a lightly floured surface and knead for 8–10 minutes, until smooth and elastic. Place in a lightly oiled bowl, cover with lightly oiled plastic wrap and let rise, in a warm place, for 1–1½ hours or until doubled in size.

3 Meanwhile, pour boiling water over the poppy seeds for the filling, then let cool. Drain thoroughly in a fine sieve. Melt the butter in a small pan, add the poppy seeds and cook, stirring, for 1–2 minutes. Remove from the heat and stir in the sugar, raisins, ground almonds, glacé fruit and cinnamon. Set aside to cool.

4 Turn the dough out onto a lightly floured surface, punch down and knead lightly. Roll out into a rectangle 14 × 10 inches. Spread the filling to within ¾ inch of the edges.

5 Roll up the dough, starting from one long edge, like a Swiss roll, tucking in the edges to seal. Place seam side down on the prepared baking sheet. Cover with lightly oiled plastic wrap and let rise, in a warm place, for 30 minutes or until doubled in size.

6 Meanwhile, preheat the oven to 375°F. Bake for 30 minutes or until golden brown. Transfer to a wire rack to cool until just warm.

7 In a small saucepan, combine the confectioners' sugar, lemon juice and enough water to make an icing stiff enough to coat the back of a spoon. Heat gently, stirring, until warm. Drizzle the icing on the loaf and sprinkle the sliced almonds on. Let cool completely, then serve sliced.

RUSSIAN POTATO BREAD

In Russia, potatoes are often used to replace some of the flour in bread recipes. They endow the bread with excellent keeping qualities.

1 Lightly grease a baking sheet. Add the potatoes to a saucepan of boiling water and cook until tender. Drain and reserve ⅔ cup of the cooking water. Mash and sieve the potatoes and let cool.

2 Combine the yeast, flours, caraway seeds and salt in a large bowl. Add the butter and rub in. Combine the reserved potato water and sieved potatoes. Gradually work this mixture into the flour mixture to form a soft dough.

3 Turn out onto a lightly floured surface and knead for 8–10 minutes until smooth and elastic. Place in a lightly oiled bowl, cover with lightly oiled plastic wrap and let rise, in a warm place, for 1 hour or until doubled in bulk.

4 Turn out onto a lightly floured surface, punch down and knead gently. Shape into a plump oval loaf, about 7 inches long. Place on the prepared baking sheet and sprinkle with a little whole-wheat flour.

5 Cover the dough with lightly oiled plastic wrap and let rise, in a warm place, for 30 minutes or until doubled in size. Meanwhile, preheat the oven to 400°F.

6 Using a sharp knife, slash the top with 3–4 diagonal cuts to make a criss-cross effect. Bake for 30–35 minutes or until golden and sounding hollow when tapped on the bottom. Transfer to a wire rack to cool.

8 ounces potatoes, peeled
and diced
¼ ounce envelope easy-blend
dried yeast
3 cups white flour
1 cup whole-wheat flour,
plus extra for sprinkling
½ teaspoon caraway
seeds, crushed
2 teaspoons salt
2 tablespoons butter

MAKES 1 LOAF

VARIATION
To make a cheese-flavored potato bread, omit the caraway seeds and knead 1 cup grated cheddar, Red Leicester or a crumbled blue cheese, such as Stilton, into the dough before shaping.

4 cups rye flour
1 teaspoon salt
¼ cup butter
¾ ounce fresh yeast
generous 1 cup lukewarm water
2 cups wheat bran

MAKES 8 CRISPBREADS

COOK'S TIP

The hole in the center of these crispbreads is a reminder of the days when breads were strung on a pole, which was hung across the rafters to dry. Make smaller crispbreads, if desired, and tie them together with bright red ribbon for an unusual Christmas gift.

KNÄCKERBRÖD

A very traditional Swedish crispbread with a lovely rye flavor.

1 Lightly grease 2 baking sheets. Preheat the oven to 450°F. Mix the rye flour and salt in a large bowl. Rub in the butter, then make a well in the center.

2 In a small bowl, mix the yeast with a little water, then stir in the remainder. Pour into the center of the flour, mix into a dough, then mix in the bran. Knead on a lightly floured surface for 5 minutes, until smooth and elastic.

3 Divide the dough into 8 equal pieces and roll each one out on a lightly floured surface to an 8-inch round.

4 Place 2 rounds on the prepared baking sheets and prick all over with a fork. Cut a hole in the center of each round, using a 1½-inch cutter.

5 Bake for 15–20 minutes or until the crispbreads are golden and crisp. Transfer to a wire rack to cool. Repeat with the remaining crispbreads.

FINNISH BARLEY BREAD

In Northern Europe breads are often made using cereals such as barley and rye, which produce very satisfying, tasty breads. This quick-to-prepare flat bread is best served warm with butter.

2 cups barley flour
1 teaspoon salt
2 teaspoons baking powder
2 tablespoons butter, melted
½ cup light cream
4 tablespoons milk

MAKES 1 SMALL LOAF

COOK'S TIPS

• This flat bread tastes very good with cottage cheese, especially cottage cheese with chives.
• For a citrusy tang, add 2–3 teaspoons finely grated lemon, lime or orange zest to the flour mixture in step 1.

1 Lightly grease a baking sheet. Preheat the oven to 400°F. Sift the dry ingredients into a bowl. Add the butter, cream and milk. Mix into a dough.

2 Turn out the dough onto a lightly floured surface and shape into a flat round about ½-inch thick.

3 Transfer to the prepared baking sheet and, using a sharp knife, lightly mark the top into 6 sections.

4 Prick the surface of the round evenly with a fork. Bake for 15–18 minutes or until pale golden. Cut into wedges and serve warm.

LUSSE BRÖD

Saint Lucia Day, December 13th, marks the beginning of Christmas in Sweden. As part of the celebrations, girls dressed in white robes wear crowns of lighted candles and walk through the village streets offering these saffron buns to the townspeople.

½ cup milk
pinch of saffron threads
3½ cups white flour
½ cup ground almonds
½ teaspoon salt
6 tablespoons sugar
1 ounce fresh yeast
½ cup lukewarm water
few drops of almond extract
¼ cup butter, softened

FOR THE GLAZE
1 egg
1 tablespoon water

MAKES 12 BUNS

VARIATION
Gently knead in 3 tablespoons currants after punching down the dough in step 4.

1 Lightly grease 2 baking sheets. Place the milk in a small saucepan and bring to a boil. Add the saffron, remove from the heat and let infuse for about 15 minutes. Meanwhile combine the flour, ground almonds, salt and sugar in a large bowl.

2 In a small bowl, mix the yeast with the water. Add the saffron liquid, yeast mixture and almond extract to the flour mixture and mix into a dough. Gradually beat in the softened butter.

3 Turn out onto a lightly floured surface and knead for 5 minutes, until smooth and elastic. Place in a lightly oiled bowl, cover with lightly oiled plastic wrap and let rise, in a warm place, for about 1 hour or until doubled in bulk.

4 Turn out onto a lightly floured surface and punch down. Divide into 12 equal pieces and make into different shapes: roll into a long rope and shape into an "S" shape; to make a star, cut a dough piece in half and roll into two ropes, cross one over the other and coil the ends; make an upturned "U" shape and coil the ends to represent curled hair; divide a dough piece in half, roll into two thin ropes and twist together.

5 Place on the prepared baking sheets, spaced well apart, cover with lightly oiled plastic wrap and let rise, in a warm place, for about 30 minutes.

6 Meanwhile, preheat the oven to 400°F. Beat the egg with the water for the glaze, and brush onto the rolls. Bake for 15 minutes or until golden. Transfer to a wire rack to cool slightly to serve warm, or cool completely to serve cold.

VÖRT LIMPA

*This festive Swedish bread is flavored with warm spices and fresh orange.
The beer and port work nicely to soften the rye taste. The added sugars also
give the yeast a little extra to feed on and help aerate and lighten the bread.
It is traditionally served with cheese.*

3 cups rye flour
3 cups white flour
½ teaspoon salt
2 tablespoons sugar
1 teaspoon grated nutmeg
1 teaspoon ground cloves
1 teaspoon ground ginger
1½ ounces fresh yeast
1¼ cups light ale
½ cup port
1 tablespoon molasses
2 tablespoons butter, melted
1 tablespoon grated orange zest
½ cup raisins
1 tablespoon malt extract, for glazing

MAKES 1 LARGE LOAF

VARIATION
This bread can be shaped into a
round or oval and baked on a baking
sheet, if preferred.

1 Lightly grease a 12 × 4-inch loaf pan.
Combine the rye and white flours, salt,
sugar, nutmeg, cloves and ginger in a
large bowl.

2 In another large bowl, using a wooden
spoon, blend the yeast into the ale until
dissolved, then stir in the port, molasses
and melted butter.

3 Gradually add the flour mixture to the
yeast liquid, beating to make a smooth
batter. Continue adding the flour a little
at a time and mixing until the mixture
forms a soft dough.

4 Turn out onto a lightly floured surface
and knead for 8–10 minutes, until smooth
and elastic. Place in a lightly oiled bowl,
cover with lightly oiled plastic wrap and
let rise, in a warm place, for 1 hour or
until doubled in size.

5 Turn out the dough onto a lightly
floured surface and punch down. Gently
knead in the orange zest and raisins.
Roll into a 12-inch square.

6 Fold the bottom third of the dough
up and the top third down, sealing the
edges. Place in the prepared pan, cover
with lightly oiled plastic wrap and let rise,
in a warm place, for 1 hour or until the
dough reaches the top of the pan.

7 Meanwhile, preheat the oven to
375°F. Bake for 35–40 minutes or
until browned. Turn out onto a wire
rack, brush with malt extract and
let cool.

BREADS OF THE AMERICAS

Yeast breads, quick breads based on baking powder, Mexican flat breads and sweet breads are all part of the diverse range found in the Americas. Traditional American ingredients such as cornmeal, molasses, corn and pumpkin provide the distinctive flavors associated with Boston brown bread, corn bread, Virginia spoon bread and pumpkin and walnut bread. San Francisco sourdough bread gains its unusual flavor not so much from its ingredients but from the fermenting process used in leavening.

SAN FRANCISCO SOURDOUGH BREAD

In San Francisco this bread is leavened using a flour and water paste, which is left to ferment with the aid of airborn yeast. The finished loaves have a moist crumb and crispy crust, and will keep for several days.

FOR THE STARTER
1/2 cup whole-wheat flour
pinch of ground cumin
1 tablespoon milk
1–2 tablespoons water
1ST REFRESHMENT
2 tablespoons water
1 cup whole-wheat flour
2ND REFRESHMENT
4 tablespoons water
1 cup white flour

FOR THE BREAD
1ST REFRESHMENT
5 tablespoons very warm water
3/4 cup all-purpose flour
2ND REFRESHMENT
3/4 cup lukewarm water
13/4–2 cups all-purpose flour

FOR THE SOURDOUGH
11/4 cups warm water
5 cups white flour
1 tablespoon salt
flour, for dusting
ice cubes, for baking

MAKES 2 ROUND LOAVES

1 Sift the flour and cumin for the starter into a bowl. Add the milk and enough water to make a firm but moist dough. Knead for 6–8 minutes to form a firm dough. Return the dough to the bowl, cover with a damp dish towel and let sit in a warm place, 75–80°F, for about 2 days. When it is ready the starter will appear moist and wrinkled and will have developed a crust.

2 Pull off the hardened crust and discard. Scoop out the moist center (about the size of a hazelnut), which will be aerated and sweet smelling, and place in a clean bowl. Mix in the water for the 1st refreshment. Gradually add the whole-wheat flour and mix into a dough.

3 Cover with plastic wrap and set in a warm place for 1–2 days. Discard the crust and gradually mix in the water for the 2nd refreshment to the starter, which by now will have a slightly sharper smell. Mix in the white flour, cover and let sit in a warm place for 8–10 hours.

4 For the bread, mix the sourdough starter with the water for the 1st refreshment. Gradually mix in the flour to form a firm dough. Knead for 6–8 minutes, until firm. Cover with a damp dish towel and let sit in a warm place for 8–12 hours or until doubled in bulk.

5 Gradually mix in the water for the 2nd refreshment, then add enough flour to form a soft, smooth elastic dough. Re-cover and let sit in a warm place for 8–12 hours. Gradually stir in the water for the sourdough, then work in the flour and salt. This will take 10–15 minutes. Turn out onto a lightly floured surface and knead until smooth and very elastic. Place in a large lightly oiled bowl, cover with lightly oiled plastic wrap and let rise, in a warm place, for 8–12 hours.

6 Divide the dough in half and shape into 2 round loaves by folding the sides over to the center and sealing.

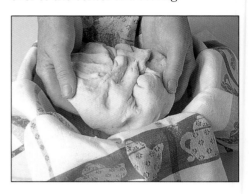

7 Place seam side up in flour-dusted *couronnes*, bowls or baskets lined with flour-dusted dish towels. Re-cover and let rise in a warm place for 4 hours.

8 Preheat the oven to 425°F. Place an empty roasting pan in the bottom of the oven. Dust 2 baking sheets with flour. Turn out the loaves seam side down on the prepared baking sheets. Using a sharp knife, cut a criss-cross pattern by slashing the top of the loaves 4–5 times in each direction.

9 Place the baking sheets in the oven and immediately drop the ice cubes into the hot roasting pan to create steam. Bake the bread for 25 minutes, then reduce the oven temperature to 400°F and bake for another 15–20 minutes or until it sounds hollow when tapped on the bottom. Transfer to wire racks to cool.

COOK'S TIP
If you want to make sourdough bread regularly, keep a small amount of the starter covered in the refrigerator. It will keep for several days. Use the starter for the 2nd refreshment, then continue as directed.

scant 1 cup yellow cornmeal
scant 1 cup white flour or
whole-wheat flour
scant 1 cup rye flour
1/2 teaspoon salt
1 teaspoon baking soda
generous 1/2 cup raisins
1/2 cup milk
1/2 cup water
1/2 cup molasses

MAKES 1 OR 2 LOAVES

COOK'S TIP
If you do not have empty coffee cans, or similar molds, cook the bread in one or two heatproof bowls of equivalent capacity.

1 Line the base of one 5-cup cylindrical metal or glass container, with greased waxed paper. Alternatively, remove the lids from two 1-pound coffee cans, wash and dry the cans thoroughly, then line with greased waxed paper.

2 Combine the cornmeal, white or whole-wheat flour, rye flour, salt, baking soda and raisins in a large bowl. Warm the milk and water in a small saucepan and stir in the molasses.

3 Add the molasses mixture to the dry ingredients and combine using a spoon until it just forms a moist dough. Do not overmix.

BOSTON BROWN BREAD

Rich, moist and dark, this bread is flavored with molasses and can include raisins. In Boston it is often served with savory baked beans.

4 Fill the container or cans with the dough; they should be about two-thirds full. Cover neatly with foil or greased waxed paper and tie securely.

5 Bring water to a depth of 2 inches to a boil in a deep, heavy saucepan large enough to accommodate the container or cans. Place a trivet in the pan, stand the container or cans on top, cover the pan and steam for 1½ hours, adding more boiling water to maintain the required level as necessary.

6 Cool the loaves for a few minutes in the container or cans, then turn them on their sides and the loaves should slip out. Serve warm, with savory dishes or Boston baked beans.

PUMPKIN AND WALNUT BREAD

—

Pumpkin, nutmeg and walnuts combine to yield a moist, tangy and slightly sweet bread with an indescribably good flavor. Serve partnered with meats or cheese, or simply lightly buttered.

1 Grease and neatly line a 8½ × 4½ inch loaf pan with parchment paper. Preheat the oven to 350°F.

2 Place the pumpkin in a saucepan, add water to cover by about 2 inches, then bring to a boil. Cover, lower the heat and simmer for 20 minutes, or until the pumpkin is very tender. Drain well, then purée in a food processor or blender. Let cool.

3 Place 1¼ cups of the purée in a large bowl. Add the sugar, nutmeg, melted butter and eggs to the purée and mix together. Sift the flour, baking powder and salt together into a large bowl and make a well in the center.

4 Add the pumpkin mixture to the center of the flour and stir until smooth. Mix in the walnuts.

1¼ pounds pumpkin, peeled, seeded
and cut into chunks
6 tablespoons sugar
1 teaspoon grated nutmeg
¼ cup butter, melted
3 eggs, lightly beaten
3 cups white flour
2 teaspoons baking powder
½ teaspoon salt
¾ cup walnuts, chopped

MAKES 1 LOAF

COOK'S TIP
If fresh pumpkin is not in season, canned puréed pumpkin in the same quantity makes a fine substitute.

5 Transfer to the prepared pan and bake for 1 hour, or until golden and starting to shrink from the sides of the pan. Turn out on to a wire rack to cool.

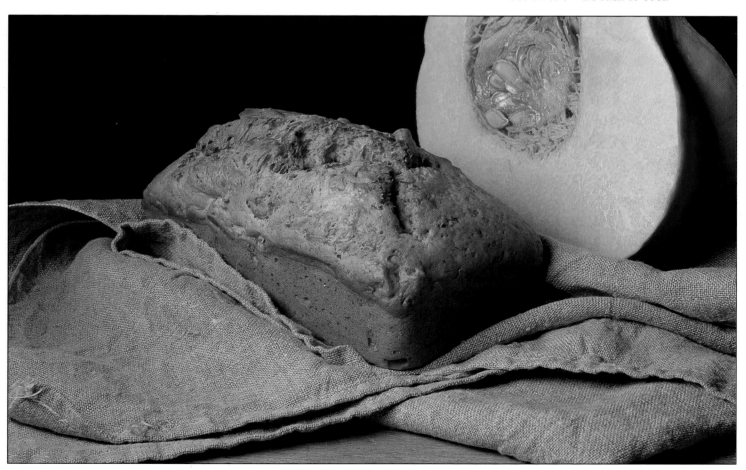

2 cups all-purpose flour
1 teaspoon salt
3/4 teaspoon baking powder
3 tablespoons lard or
solid vegetable shortening
2/3 cup warm water

MAKES 12 TORTILLAS

3/4 cup white flour
1 1/2 cups yellow cornmeal
1 teaspoon salt
1 1/2 tablespoons baking powder
1 tablespoon sugar
4 tablespoons butter, melted
1 cup milk
3 eggs
scant 1 1/4 cups canned corn, drained

MAKES 1 LARGE LOAF

WHEAT TORTILLAS

Tortillas are the staple flat bread in Mexico, where they are often made from masa harina, a flour milled from corn. These soft wheat tortillas are also popular in the southwestern part of the United States.

1 Mix the flour, salt and baking powder in a bowl. Rub in the fat, stir in the water and knead lightly until you have a soft dough. Cover with plastic wrap and let rest for 15 minutes. Divide into 12 equal pieces and shape into balls. Roll out on a lightly floured surface into 6–7-inch rounds. Re-cover to keep moist.

2 Heat a heavy frying pan or griddle, add one tortilla and cook for 1 1/2–2 minutes, turning over as soon as the surface starts to bubble. It should stay flexible. Remove from the pan and wrap in a dish towel to keep warm while cooking the remaining tortillas in the same way.

DOUBLE CORN BREAD

In the American South, corn bread is made with white cornmeal and is fairly flat, while in the North it is thicker and made with yellow cornmeal. Whatever the version, it's delicious—this recipe combines yellow cornmeal with sweet corn. It is great served warm, cut into wedges and buttered.

1 Preheat the oven to 400°F. Grease and line an 8 1/2-inch round cake pan with baking parchment. Sift the flour, cornmeal, salt and baking powder together into a large bowl. Stir in the sugar and make a well in the center.

3 Using a wooden spoon, stir the corn quickly into the mixture. Pour into the prepared pan and bake for 20–25 minutes or until a metal skewer inserted into the center comes out clean.

2 Combine the melted butter, milk and eggs. Add to the center of the flour mixture and beat until just combined.

4 Invert the bread onto a wire rack and lift off the lining paper. Cool slightly. Serve warm, cut into wedges.

VIRGINIA SPOON BREAD

1³/4 cups milk
²/3 cup cornmeal
1 tablespoon butter
³/4 cup grated sharp cheddar cheese
1 garlic clove
3 eggs, separated
1/2 cup corn
kernels (optional)
salt and freshly ground black pepper

MAKES 1 LARGE LOAF

Spoon bread is a traditional dish from the southern United States which, according to legend, originated when too much water was added to a corn bread batter and the baked bread had to be spooned out of the pan. Served hot from the oven, this ethereally light offering—enhanced with cheddar cheese and a hint of garlic—is delicious.

VARIATIONS
Add 4 ounces fried chopped bacon or 1–2 teaspoons finely chopped green chili for different flavored spoon breads.

1 Preheat the oven to 350°F. Grease a 6-cup soufflé dish.

2 Place the milk in a large heavy saucepan. Heat gently, then gradually add the cornmeal, stirring. Add salt and slowly bring to a boil, stirring constantly. Cook for 5–10 minutes, stirring frequently, until thick and smooth.

3 Remove from the heat and stir in the butter, cheddar cheese, garlic and egg yolks. Season to taste.

4 In a bowl, whisk the egg whites until they form soft peaks. Stir one-quarter into the cornmeal mixture and then gently fold in the remainder. Fold in the well-drained corn, if using.

5 Spoon the mixture into the prepared soufflé dish and bake for 45–50 minutes or until puffed and beginning to brown. Serve immediately.

COOK'S TIPS
• Use a perfectly clean bowl and whisk for whisking the egg whites, and make sure it is free of grease by washing and drying thoroughly, then wiping out with a little lemon juice.
• If any shell drops in with the egg, scoop it out with another, larger piece of shell.

NEW ENGLAND FANTANS

*These fantail rolls look stylish and are so versatile that they are equally
suitable for a simple snack or a gourmet dinner party!*

1 Grease a muffin sheet with 3-inch cups or foil cases. Mix the yeast with the buttermilk and sugar and then let stand for 15 minutes.

2 In a saucepan, heat the milk with 3 tablespoons of the butter until the butter has melted. Cool until lukewarm.

3 Sift the flour and salt together into a large bowl. Add the yeast mixture, milk mixture and egg and mix into a soft dough. Turn out onto a lightly floured surface and knead for 5–8 minutes, until smooth and elastic. Place in a lightly oiled bowl, cover with lightly oiled plastic wrap and let rise, in a warm place, for about 1 hour, until doubled in size.

4 Turn out onto a lightly floured surface, punch down and knead until smooth and elastic. Roll into an oblong measuring 18 × 12 inches and about 1/4-inch thick. Melt the remaining butter, brush it over the dough and cut it lengthwise into 5 equal strips. Stack on top of each other and cut across into 9 equal 2-inch strips.

5 Pinch one side of each layered strip together, then place pinched side down into a prepared muffin cup or foil case. Cover with lightly oiled plastic wrap and let rise, in a warm place, for 30–40 minutes or until the fantans have almost doubled in size. Meanwhile, preheat the oven to 400°F. Bake for 20 minutes or until golden. Turn out onto a wire rack to cool.

1/2 ounce fresh yeast
5 tablespoons buttermilk, at room
temperature
2 teaspoons sugar
5 tablespoons milk
5 tablespoons butter
3 1/4 cups white flour
1 teaspoon salt
1 egg, lightly beaten

MAKES 9 ROLLS

VARIATION
To make cinnamon-spiced Fantans, add 1 teaspoon ground cinnamon to the remaining butter in step 4 before brushing over the dough strips. Sprinkle the rolls with a little confectioners' sugar as soon as they come out of the oven, then let cool before serving.

BREADS OF INDIA AND THE MIDDLE EAST

Chapatis, pooris, rotis and naan are typical unleavened Indian flat breads. Chiles, herbs and spices are popular additions and cooking methods range from baking in a traditional clay tandoor to frying in oil. The tradition of baking flat breads continues into the Middle East, although their specialties—crisp lavash, onion breads and barbari—include yeast. All these breads are perfect for serving with soups or dips.

BHATURAS

—

*These light, fluffy leavened breads, made with semolina and flour and
flavored with butter and yogurt, taste delicious served warm.*

1/2 ounce fresh yeast
1 teaspoon sugar
1/2 cup lukewarm water
1 3/4 cups all-purpose flour
1/2 cup semolina
1/2 teaspoon salt
1 tablespoon butter or ghee
2 tablespoons plain yogurt
oil, for frying

MAKES 10 BHATURAS

COOK'S TIP
Ghee can be found in Asian and
Indian supermarkets, however, it is
easy to make at home. Melt unsalted
butter in a heavy-bottomed pan over
low heat. Simmer very gently until the
residue changes to a light golden
color, then leave to cool. Strain
through cheesecloth before using.

1 Mix the yeast with the sugar and
water in a bowl. Sift the flour into a
large bowl and stir in the semolina and
salt. Rub in the butter or ghee.

2 Add the yeast mixture and yogurt and
mix to a dough. Turn out on to a lightly
floured surface and knead for
10 minutes until smooth and elastic.

3 Place in a lightly oiled bowl, cover
with lightly oiled plastic wrap and let
rise, in a warm place, for about 1 hour,
or until doubled in bulk.

4 Turn out on to a lightly floured surface
and punch down. Divide into 10 equal
pieces and shape each one into a ball.
Flatten into disks with the palm of your
hand. Roll out on a lightly floured
surface into 5-inch rounds.

5 Heat oil to a depth of 1/2-inch in a
deep frying pan and slide one bhatura
into the oil. Fry for about 1 minute,
turning over after 30 seconds, then
drain on paper towels. Keep warm in a
low oven while frying the remaining
bhaturas. Serve warm.

TANDOORI ROTIS

There are numerous varieties of breads in India, most of them unleavened. This one, as its name suggests, would normally be baked in a tandoor—a clay oven which is heated with charcoal or wood. The oven becomes extremely hot, cooking the bread in minutes.

3 cups atta *or fine whole-wheat flour*
1 teaspoon salt
1 cup water
2–3 tablespoons melted ghee or butter, for brushing

MAKES 6 ROTIS

COOK'S TIP
The rotis are ready when light brown bubbles appear on the surface.

1 Sift the flour and salt into a large bowl. Add the water and mix to a soft dough. Knead on a lightly floured surface for 3–4 minutes until smooth. Place in a lightly oiled bowl, cover with lightly oiled plastic wrap; let rest for 1 hour.

2 Turn out on to a lightly floured surface. Divide the dough into 6 pieces and shape each piece into a ball. Press out into a larger round with the palm of your hand, cover with lightly oiled plastic wrap and let rest for 10 minutes.

3 Meanwhile, preheat the oven to 450°F. Place 3 baking sheets in the oven to heat. Roll the rotis into 6-inch rounds, place 2 on each baking sheet and bake for 8–10 minutes. Brush with ghee or butter and serve warm.

NAAN

From the Caucasus through the Punjab region of northwest India and beyond, all serve these leavened breads. Traditionally cooked in a very hot clay oven known as a tandoor, naan are usually eaten with dry meat or vegetable dishes, such as tandoori.

2 cups unbleached white bread flour
1/2 teaspoon salt
1/2 ounce fresh yeast
4 tablespoons lukewarm milk
1 tablespoon vegetable oil
2 tablespoons plain yogurt
1 egg
2–3 tablespoons melted ghee or
butter, for brushing

MAKES 3 NAAN

VARIATIONS
You can flavor naan in numerous different ways:
• To make spicy naan, add 1 teaspoon each ground coriander and ground cumin to the flour in step 1. If you would like the naan to be extra fiery, add 1/2–1 teaspoon hot chile powder.
• To make cardamom-flavored naan, lightly crush the seeds from 4–5 green cardamom pods and add to the flour in step 1.
• To make poppy seed naan, brush the rolled-out naan with a little ghee and sprinkle with poppy seeds. Press lightly to make sure that they stick.
• To make peppered naan, brush the rolled-out naan with a little ghee and dust generously with coarsely ground black pepper.
• To make onion-flavored naan, add 1/2 cup finely chopped or coarsely grated onion to the dough in step 2. You may need to reduce the amount of egg if the onion is very moist to prevent making the dough too soft.
• To make whole-wheat naan, substitute whole-wheat bread flour for some or all of the white flour.

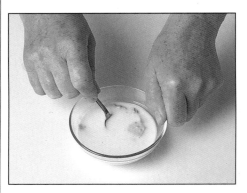

1 Sift the flour and salt together into a large bowl. In a smaller bowl, cream the yeast with the milk. Set aside for 15 minutes.

2 Add the yeast mixture, oil, yogurt and egg to the flour and mix to a soft dough.

3 Turn out the dough on to a lightly floured surface and knead for about 10 minutes until smooth and elastic. Place in a lightly oiled bowl, cover with lightly oiled plastic wrap and let rise, in a warm place, for 45 minutes, or until doubled in bulk.

4 Preheat the oven to its highest setting, at least 450°F. Place 3 heavy baking sheets in the oven to heat.

5 Turn the dough out on to a lightly floured surface and punch down. Divide into 3 equal pieces and shape into balls.

6 Cover two of the balls of dough with oiled plastic wrap and roll out the third into a teardrop shape about 10 inches long, 5 inches wide and with a thickness of about 1/4–1/3 inch.

7 Preheat the broiler on its highest setting. Meanwhile, place the naan on the hot baking sheets and bake for 3–4 minutes, or until puffed up.

8 Remove the naan from the oven and place under the hot broiler for a few seconds, or until the top of the naan browns slightly. Wrap the cooked naan in a dish towel to keep warm while rolling out and cooking the remaining naan. Brush with melted ghee or butter and serve warm.

COOK'S TIP
To help the naan dough to puff up and brown, place the baking sheets in an oven preheated to the maximum temperature for at least 10 minutes before baking to ensure that they are hot. Preheat the broiler while the naan are baking.

*1 cup unbleached
all-purpose flour
1 cup whole-wheat flour
1/2 teaspoon salt
1/2 teaspoon chile powder (optional)
2 tablespoons vegetable oil
scant 1/2 cup water
oil, for frying*

MAKES 12 POORIS

VARIATION

To make spinach-flavored pooris, thaw 2 ounces frozen chopped spinach, drain it well and add it to the dough with a little grated fresh ginger root and 1/2 teaspoon ground cumin.

POORIS

Pooris are small disks of dough that when fried, puff up into light airy breads. They will melt in your mouth!

1 Sift the flours, salt and chile powder, if using, into a large bowl. Add the vegetable oil then add sufficient water to mix to a dough. Turn out on to a lightly floured surface and knead for 8–10 minutes until smooth.

2 Place in a lightly oiled bowl and cover with lightly oiled plastic wrap. Let rest for 30 minutes.

3 Turn out on to a lightly floured surface. Divide the dough into 12 equal pieces. Keeping the rest of the dough covered, roll one piece into a 5-inch round. Repeat with the remaining dough. Stack the pooris, layered between plastic wrap, to keep moist.

4 Heat oil to a depth of 1 inch in a deep frying pan to 350°F. Using a spatula, lift one poori and gently slide it into the oil; it will sink but return to the surface and begin to sizzle. Gently press the poori into the oil. It will puff up. Turn over after a few seconds and cook for 20–30 seconds.

5 Remove the poori from the pan and drain on paper towels. Keep warm in a low oven while cooking the remaining pooris. Serve warm.

---

*1 1/2 cups atta or whole-wheat flour
1/2 teaspoon salt
scant scant 1/2 cup water
1 teaspoon vegetable oil
melted ghee or butter, for brushing
(optional)*

MAKES 6 CHAPATIS

COOK'S TIP

Atta or *ata* is a very fine whole-wheat flour, which is only found in Indian stores and supermarkets. It is sometimes simply labeled chapati flour. *Atta* can also be used for making rotis and other Indian flat breads.

1 Sift the flour and salt into a bowl. Add the water and mix to a soft dough. Knead in the oil, then turn out on to a lightly floured surface.

CHAPATIS

These chewy, unleavened breads are eaten throughout Northern India. They are usually served as an accompaniment to spicy dishes.

2 Knead for 5–6 minutes until smooth. Place in a lightly oiled bowl, cover with a damp dish towel and let rest for 30 minutes. Turn out on to a floured surface. Divide the dough into 6 equal pieces. Shape each piece into a ball.

3 Press the dough into a larger round with the palm of your hand, then roll into a 5-inch round. Stack, layered between plastic wrap, to keep moist.

4 Heat a griddle or heavy-based frying pan over a medium heat for a few minutes until hot. Take one chapati, brush off any excess flour, and place on the griddle. Cook for 30–60 seconds, or until the top begins to bubble and white specks appear on the underside.

5 Turn the chapati over using a spatula and cook for a further 30 seconds. Remove from the pan and keep warm, layered between a folded dish towel, while cooking the remaining chapatis. If you like, the chapatis can be brushed lightly with melted ghee or butter immediately after cooking. Serve warm.

MISSI ROTIS

1 cup gram flour
1 cup whole-wheat flour
1 green chile, seeded and chopped
1/2 onion, finely chopped
1 tablespoon chopped fresh cilantro
1/2 teaspoon ground turmeric
1/2 teaspoon salt
1 tablespoon oil or melted butter
1/2–2/3 cup lukewarm water
2–3 tablespoons melted butter
or ghee

MAKES 4 ROTIS

VARIATION
Use 1/4–1/2 teaspoon chile powder in
place of the fresh chile.

These flavor-packed unleavened breads are eaten in northern India. They are made with gram flour—grams or chana dhal are a variety of chickpea, which are milled to make this gluten-free flour.

1 Mix the flours, chile, onion, cilantro, turmeric and salt together in a large bowl. Stir in the 1 tablespoon oil or melted butter.

2 Mix in sufficient water to make a pliable soft dough. Turn out the dough on to a lightly floured surface and knead until smooth.

3 Place in a lightly oiled bowl, cover with lightly oiled plastic wrap and let rest for 1 hour.

4 Turn the dough out on to a lightly floured surface. Divide into 4 equal pieces and shape into balls. Roll out each ball into a thick round 6–7 inches in diameter.

5 Heat a griddle or heavy-based frying pan over a medium heat for a few minutes until hot.

6 Brush both sides of one roti with the melted butter or ghee. Add it to the griddle or frying pan and cook for about 2 minutes, turning after 1 minute. Brush the cooked roti lightly with melted butter or ghee again, slide it on to a plate and keep warm in a low oven while cooking the remaining rotis in the same way. Serve the rotis warm.

LAVASH

Thin and crispy, this flat bread is universally eaten throughout the Middle East. It's ideal for serving with soups and starters, and can be made in any size and broken into pieces as desired.

2 1/2 cups unbleached white
bread flour
1 1/2 cups whole-wheat flour
1 teaspoon salt
1/2 ounce fresh yeast
1 cup lukewarm water
4 tablespoons plain yogurt or milk

MAKES 10 LAVASH

1 Sift the white and whole-wheat flours and salt together into a large bowl and make a well in the center. Mix the yeast with half the lukewarm water until creamy, then stir in the remaining water.

2 Add the yeast mixture and yogurt or milk to the center of the flour and mix to a soft dough. Turn out on to a lightly floured surface and knead for 8–10 minutes until smooth and elastic. Place in a lightly oiled bowl, cover with lightly oiled plastic wrap and let rise, in a warm place, for about 1 hour, or until doubled in bulk. Punch down the dough, re-cover with lightly oiled plastic wrap and let rise for 30 minutes.

3 Turn the dough back out on to a lightly floured surface. Punch down gently and divide into 10 equal pieces. Shape into balls, then flatten into disks with the palm of your hand. Cover and let rest for 5 minutes. Meanwhile, preheat the oven to the maximum temperature – at least 450°F. Place 3 or 4 baking sheets in the oven to heat.

4 Roll the dough as thinly as possible, then lift it over the backs of your hands and gently stretch and turn the dough. Let rest in between rolling for a few minutes if necessary to avoid tearing.

5 As soon as they are ready, place 4 lavash on the baking sheets and bake for 6–8 minutes, or until starting to brown. Stack the remaining uncooked lavash, layered between plastic wrap or waxed paper, and cover, to keep moist. Transfer to a wire rack to cool and cook the remaining lavash.

4 cups unbleached white bread flour
1 teaspoon salt
3/4 ounce fresh yeast
scant 1 1/4 cups lukewarm water

FOR THE TOPPING
4 tablespoons finely chopped onion
1 teaspoon ground cumin
2 teaspoons ground coriander
2 teaspoons chopped fresh mint
2 tablespoons olive oil

MAKES 8 BREADS

COOK'S TIP
If you haven't any fresh mint to hand, then add 1 tablespoon dried mint. Use the freeze-dried variety if you can as it has much more flavor.

SYRIAN ONION BREAD

The basic Arab breads of the Levant and Gulf have traditionally been made with a finely ground whole-wheat flour similar to chapati flour, but now are being made with white flour as well. This Syrian version has a tasty, aromatic topping.

1 Lightly flour 2 baking sheets. Sift the flour and salt together into a large bowl and make a well in the center. Cream the yeast with a little of the water, then mix in the remainder.

2 Add the yeast mixture to the center of the flour and mix to a firm dough. Turn out on to a lightly floured surface and knead for 8–10 minutes until smooth and elastic.

3 Place in a lightly oiled bowl, cover with lightly oiled plastic wrap and leave to rise, in a warm place, for about 1 hour, or until doubled in size.

4 Punch down the dough and turn out on to a lightly floured surface. Divide into 8 equal pieces and roll into 5–6-inch rounds. Make them slightly concave. Prick all over and space well apart on the baking sheets. Cover with lightly oiled plastic wrap and let rise for 15–20 minutes.

5 Meanwhile, preheat the oven to 400°F. Mix the chopped onion, ground cumin, ground coriander and chopped mint in a bowl. Brush the breads with the olive oil for the topping, sprinkle them evenly with the spicy onion mixture and bake for 15–20 minutes. Serve the onion breads warm.

BARBARI

*These small Iranian flat breads can be made in a variety of sizes. For a
change, make two large breads and break off pieces to scoop up dips.*

1 Lightly dust 2 baking sheets with flour.
Sift the flour and salt together into a
bowl and make a well in the center.

3 Place in a lightly oiled bowl, cover
with lightly oiled plastic wrap and let
rise for 45–60 minutes, or until doubled.

2 cups unbleached white bread flour
1 teaspoon salt
1/2 ounce fresh yeast
scant 2/3 cup lukewarm water
oil, for brushing

MAKES 6 BARBARI

2 Mix the yeast with the water. Pour
into the center of the flour, sprinkle a
little flour over and leave in a warm
place for 15 minutes. Mix to a dough,
then turn out on to a lightly floured
surface and knead for 8–10 minutes
until smooth and elastic.

4 Punch down the dough and turn out
on to a lightly floured surface. Divide
into 6 equal pieces and shape into
rectangles. Roll each one out to about
4 × 2 inches and about 1/2-inch thick.
Space well apart on the baking sheets,
and make four slashes in the tops.

VARIATION
Sprinkle with sesame or caraway
seeds before baking.

5 Cover the breads with lightly oiled
plastic wrap and let rise, in a warm
place, for 20 minutes. Meanwhile,
preheat the oven to 400°F. Brush
the breads with oil and bake for
12–15 minutes, or until pale golden.
Serve warm.

INDEX

PUBLISHER'S ACKNOWLEDGEMENTS

The Publishers would like to thank Jo Lethaby and
Jenni Fleetwood for their skilful editing.
All recipe pictures and chapter openers are by
Nicki Dowey. The pictures on pages 6–31 are
by Amanda Heywood, except for the following
that have been reproduced with the kind
permission of those listed:
p. 6t, p. 7t, and p. 14b Maison Blanc Limited;
p. 7b Jan Suttle/Life File.